PRIMER OF EQUAL EMPLOYMENT OPPORTUNITY

HOWARD J. ANDERSON
Senior Editor for Labor Services
The Bureau of National Affairs, Inc.

Published 1978 by
THE BUREAU OF NATIONAL AFFAIRS, INC.
WASHINGTON, D.C.

Library of Congress Cataloging in Publication Data
Anderson, Howard J.
    Primer of equal employment opportunity.
    Includes index.
    1. Discrimination in employment—Law and
legislation—United States I. Title.
KF3464.A953   344'.73'01133   77-16374
ISBN 0-87179-269-9

Printed in the United States of America
International Standard Book Number: 0-87179-269-9

CONTENTS

68912
12
8

THE LAW OF EQUAL EMPLOYMENT OPPORTUNITY: AN OVERVIEW

Discrimination in employment based on race, color, religion, sex, or national origin was made unlawful by Title VII of the Civil Rights Act of 1964. In 1967, employment discrimination based on age was forbidden. In 1973, handicapped status was added to the list; then in 1974, an employment preference was provided for disabled veterans and veterans of the Vietnam era.

The results have been a proliferation of government agencies engaged in policing employment discrimination, burgeoning caseloads, and development of an entire new body of law. The principal agency involved, the Equal Employment Opportunity Commission, has had a case backlog estimated to exceed 100,000.

LAWS, ORDERS INVOLVED

The problem of complying with the obligation of equal employment opportunity is complicated by the myriad of laws, orders, and regulations. They include:

► *Title VII of the Civil Rights Act of 1964,* which forbade employment or membership discrimination by employer, employment agencies, and unions on the basis of race, color, religion, sex, or national origin. It also established the Equal Employment Opportunity Commission, but it gave the Commission no enforcement powers.

► *The Equal Employment Opportunity Act of 1972,* which amended Title VII to broaden its coverage and give the Commission (EEOC) power to bring enforcement actions in the courts.

► *The Civil Rights Acts of 1866* (42 U.S.C. Sec. 1981), which in the last few years has been used in actions to redress employment discrimination based on race, alienage, and probably national origin. It gives all persons the same contractual rights as "white citizens." Section 1981 does not apply to discrimination based on sex.

1

► *The Civil Rights Act of 1871* (42 U.S.C. Sec. 1983), which applies to persons acting "under color of state law" to deprive others of federal rights, including equal employment opportunity. But in a case decided by the Supreme Court in 1977, it was held that an Ohio law barring unemployment compensation to workers laid off because of a strike violates neither Section 1983 nor the Fourteenth Amendment. (Ohio Bureau of Employment Services v. Godoy)

► *The Age Discrimination in Employment Act,* which makes it unlawful to discriminate against employees or applicants for employment who are between 40 and 65 years of age. In 1978, Congress amended the Act to raise the top age to 70, effective April 6, 1978, for employees then under age 65 and effective January 1, 1979, for employees then between the ages of 65 and 69, subject to an exception for employees covered by collective bargaining contracts. The Act placed the administration of the provisions in the Wage-Hour Division of the Labor Department. But a reorganization plan proposed by the President and not disapproved by Congress transferred administration to EEOC, effective July 1, 1979.

► *The Equal Pay Act of 1963,* which makes it unlawful to pay a different rate to members of the other sex for equal work on jobs that require equal skill, effort, and responsibility under similar working conditions in the same establishment. Its coverage is the same as that of the Fair Labor Standards Act. The Act gave the responsibility for administering and enforcing the provisions to the Wage-Hour Division of the Labor Department. But a reorganization plan proposed by the President and not disapproved by Congress transferred this responsibility to EEOC, effective July 1, 1979.

► *The National Labor Relations Act,* which has been invoked under the doctrine of fair representation where there was employment discrimination caused by unions. But in 1977, the NLRB held that it would not deny a union certification as a collective bargaining representative because of charges that it engaged in racial discrimination. It earlier had held that it would not police employment discrimination based on race by employers.

► *Executive Order 11246* (as amended by Executive Order 11375), which forbids employment discrimination based on race, color, religion, sex, or national origin by first- and second-tier government contractors whose contracts are in amounts exceeding $10,000.

▶ *State fair employment practice statutes,* which are found in all but five of the states (Alabama, Arkansas, Louisiana, Mississippi, and North Dakota), but both the coverage and the administrative and substantive provisions vary widely.

▶ *Municipal human relations ordinances,* which have been adopted by about 70 cities, some in states in which there is no state fair employment practice law. Like the state laws, these ordinances vary widely.

▶ *The Rehabilitation Act of 1973,* which requires federal contractors to take affirmative action to employ and promote qualified handicapped persons. This law is administered by the Labor Department.

▶ *Title VI of the Civil Rights Acts of 1964,* which forbids discrimination in employment based on race, color, or national origin in all programs or activities that receive federal financial assistance. Title VI does not specifically bar employment discrimination based on sex, but some of the agencies have barred such discrimination in their regulations.

▶ *The Vietnam Era Veterans Readjustment Assistance Act,* which requires employers with government contracts of $10,000 or more to take affirmative action to employ and advance disabled veterans and qualified veterans of the Vietnam era.

▶ *The General Revenue Sharing Act,* which imposes an obligation on state and local governments receiving federal revenue sharing not to discriminate in employment on the basis of race, color, national origin, sex, religion, age, or handicapped status.

MULTIPLE FORUMS AND REMEDIES

In addition to the laws, orders, and ordinances, collective bargaining contracts also play a role in enforcing equal employment opportunity.

Moreover, the courts have taken the position that the contract and the various statutory remedies are independent. So an aggrieved person may pursue his claim in more than one forum, and if he loses in one, he may sue in another. Thus, the Supreme Court held in Alexander v. Gardner-Denver Co. that an employee who had pursued a claim of discrimination through the grievance-arbitration procedure under a collective bargaining agreement and lost was not barred from suing in court under Title VII. Rights under Title VII are distinctly separate in nature from rights under a collective bargaining contract, the Court said. (7 FEP Cases 81)

WHO IS COVERED BY TITLE VII

The coverage of Title VII extends about as far as it is possible for Congress to reach under its authority to regulate interstate commerce. The coverage depends on a series of definitions. All were included in the 1964 Act, but some were modified by the 1972 amendments.

A key definition is that of "industry affecting commerce"—the basic test of coverage. The definition is in two parts. First, "commerce" is defined broadly to include trade, transportation, or communication among the states or between a state and a point outside it. Second, the phrase "affecting commerce" is defined the same way it is in the 1959 Landrum-Griffin Act to include any activity that would hinder or obstruct commerce.

Under these definitions, the coverage of Title VII is broader than that of the Fair Labor Standards Act, which covers employees "engaged in commerce" or in the "production of goods for commerce." Title VII also has a broader coverage than the Taft-Hartley Act, since the NLRB has set dollar-volume standards for assertion of jurisdiction.

COVERAGE OF EMPLOYERS

The coverage of employers under the 1972 Act is governed by three definitions. They are:

Person, which was broadened by the 1972 amendments to include state and local governments, governmental agencies, and political subdivisions.

Employer, which also was broadened by the 1972 amendments to include state and local governments, governmental agencies, and political subdivisions. But the definition does not include the U.S. Government, corporations wholly owned by the Government, or departments of the District of Columbia that are subject to competitive service.

4

Persons in an industry affecting commerce, which is not limited to a person with flesh and blood. It also includes the usual organizations that people establish to further a common purpose—corporations, associations, labor unions, mutual companies, joint stock companies, trusts, and unincorporated associations. Moreover, legal representatives are "persons," and so are trustees, trustees in bankruptcy, and receivers.

NUMBER-OF-EMPLOYEES TEST

Since March 24, 1973, an employer has been required to have 15 or more employees to be covered by Title VII. Under the 1964 Act, the number of employees required for coverage was established on a reducing scale, beginning with 100 in 1965 and dropping to 25 in 1968.

To be covered under this test, the employer must have the required number of employees on each working day of 20 or more calendar weeks in the current or preceding calendar year. Once this requirement is met, it is satisfied for two calendar years.

MULTIPLE ESTABLISHMENTS

In determining whether nominally separate business entities meet the jurisdictional requirements of Title VII when combined, but not when treated separately, the EEOC applies the tests used by the NLRB in determining coverage under the Taft-Hartley Act. These tests are:

► Interrelation of operations;

► Common management;

► Centralized control of labor relations; and

► Common ownership.

GOVERNMENT EMPLOYEES

Under the 1972 amendments, the coverage of Title VII was extended to state and local governments, government agencies, political subdivisions, and departments and agencies of the District of Columbia, except those subject to competitive service.

There is an exception. Excluded from coverage are elected officials, their personal assistants, and their immediate advisers.

Federal employees were not covered by the 1964 Act. But the 1972 amendments added a new section to make clear the obligation of the Federal Government not to discriminate on the basis of race, color, sex, religion, or national origin in its personnel actions.

During its 1975-1976 Term, the Supreme Court handed down a number of rulings relating to protection against employment discrimination for government employees under the Constitution, Title VII, and 42 U.S.C. Sec. 1981 (1866 Act). The Court held:

► The 1972 amendments extending the coverage of Title VII to the states are constitutional. The Court added that the Eleventh Amendment does not bar an award of attorneys' fees and retroactive retirement benefits to employees who proved in their Title VII action that a state retirement system had discriminated against them because of their sex. (Fitzpatrick v. Bitzer, 12 FEP Cases 1586) This case took on added significance in view of the Court's holding in the National League of Cities case that the 1974 amendments to the Fair Labor Standards Act that extended minimum-wage and overtime-pay protection to almost all nonsupervisory employees of state and local governments violated the Constitution. (22 WH Cases 1064)

► A personnel test that excludes a disproportionately large number of black applicants for police officer positions does not violate due process requirements solely by reason of its racially disproportionate impact. This was the Washington v. Davis case. (12 FEP Cases 1415)

► Section 717 of the Civil Rights Act of 1964 is the exclusive individual remedy available to a U.S. Government employee who charges job-related racial discrimination. (Brown v. GSA, 12 FEP Cases 1361)

► A federal employee who files a Section 717 action is entitled to a trial *de novo,* not just to review of the record compiled in the administrative proceeding on his claim. (Chandler v. Roudebush, 12 FEP Cases 1368)

► A U.S. Civil Service regulation excluding all aliens from all civil service positions is unconstitutional. The holding was handed down in the Wong and Ramos cases. (Hampton v. Wong, 12 FEP Cases 1377; U.S. Civil Service Commission v. Ramos, 12 FEP Cases 1446) Massachusetts may require that state police officers retire at age 50, and Louisiana may require that nonelected, nonappointed state civil service employees retire at age 65. (Massachusetts Board of Retirement v. Murgia, 12 FEP Cases 1569; Cannon v. Guste, 11 FEP Cases 715)

WHO IS AN EMPLOYEE

An "employee" is defined broadly in Title VII as an individual employed by an employer. Although this would appear to exclude applicants for employment, the omission appears to be without significance, since it is unlawful to refuse to hire "any individual" on the basis of race, color, religion, sex, or national origin.

As pointed out above, there is an exemption for persons elected to public office in any state or political subdivision by the qualified voters. The exemption also extends to persons chosen by such elected officials to be on their personal staffs, appointees on the policy-making level, or immediate advisers with respect to the exercise of the constitutional or legal powers of the office. The exemption does not extend to employees subject to the civil service laws of a state government, governmental agency, or political subdivision.

In contrast to the Taft-Hartley Act, Title VII does not exclude supervisors from the definition of an "employee." Nor are executive, administrative, or professional employees exempted, as they are under the Fair Labor Standards Act.

COVERAGE OF LABOR ORGANIZATIONS

Title VII's coverage of labor organizations is complicated, since a union may be covered both as an employer and a labor organization, and the definition of a "labor organization" is very broad and complex. To be covered as an *employer,* a union must have 15 or more employees. To be covered as a *labor organization,* it must have 15 or more members.

The definition of a "labor organization" is virtually the same as that in the Landrum-Griffin Act. It includes "any organization in which employees participate" to deal with their employer on the usual subjects of collective bargaining.

So coverage is not limited to local unions. It also extends to national and international unions and collateral bodies, such as councils, joint boards, and state or local central bodies.

A union must also be "engaged in an industry affecting commerce" to be covered by Title VII. It may meet this test on two bases: (1) by meeting the number-of-members—15—test; or (2) by maintaining a hiring hall or hiring office that brings "employers and employees together."

If a union meets one of these tests, it then is covered if it meets one of these three additional tests:

► It is certified as a bargaining representative under the National Labor Relations Act or the Railway Labor Act.

► It is recognized as a bargaining representative by an employer covered by Title VII.

► It has some formal relationship with a labor organization covered by Title VII as a chartered or joint interest organization.

HIRING HALLS, APPRENTICESHIP

The 1964 Act covered joint labor-management committees that control apprenticeship or other training or retraining programs. The provisions were amended in 1972 to make it unlawful for such committees to retaliate against any person for enforcing his rights under the Act or to advertise or post a notice that indicates any preference, limitation, specification, or discrimination based on race, color, religion, sex, or national origin. There is an exception, however, where religion, sex, or national origin is a bona fide occupational qualification for employment. The exception does not apply to race or color.

In 1972, the Act was also amended to make hiring halls or offices explicitly subject to Title VII without regard to the number-of-members test.

COVERAGE OF EMPLOYMENT AGENCIES

The definition of an "employment agency" was broadened by the 1974 amendments to cover any person regularly undertaking with or without compensation to procure employees for an employer or to procure for employees opportunities to work for an employer.

Coverage also extends to the U.S. Employment Service and state and local employment services that receive federal assistance.

EXEMPTIONS FROM THE ACT

The 1972 amendments to Title VII deleted one exemption, enlarged one, and added one. Here are the changes:

► The 1964 exemption for educational institutions with respect to individuals whose work involves educational activities was eliminated.

► The original exemption for religious corporations, associations, or societies with respect to individuals whose work involves the religious aspects of the organization was broadened to include all activities of such organizations, not merely the religious activities. But the exemption applies only to discrimination based on religion. It does not apply to discrimination based on race, color, sex, or national origin.

► The new coverage of state and local governments, as noted above, contains an exemption for elected officials, their personal assistants, and their immediate advisers.

UNCHANGED EXEMPTIONS

A number of exemptions were carried over unchanged from the 1964 Act. They included:

► An exemption giving Indians living on or near a reservation preference in employment by businesses on or near the reservation.

► An exemption for bona fide, tax-exempt private clubs, such clubs being excluded from the definition of an "employer" under Title VII.

► An exemption for employers otherwise covered with respect to aliens they employ in foreign countries.

► An exemption for employees of an employer who is subject to a government security program where the employees do not have security clearance.

► An exemption that denies Title VII protection to any individual who "is a member of the Communist Party of the U.S. or of any other organization required to register as a Communist-Action or Communist-front organization by a final order of the Subversive Activities Control Board." A proposed exemption to exclude atheists from Title VII protection was defeated, however.

► An exemption where religion, sex, or national origin is a bona fide occupational qualification reasonably necessary to the normal operation of the particular business.

DISCRIMINATION BY EMPLOYERS ON THE BASIS OF RACE

Title VII makes it an unlawful employment practice for an employer to discriminate against an individual because of his race, color, religion, sex, or national origin with respect to compensation, terms, conditions, or privileges of employment. Discrimination by employment agencies and unions, insofar as it differs from that by employers, is discussed below under the headings: "Discrimination by Employment Agencies" and "Discrimination by Unions."

In many cases, the rules on discrimination on the basis of race overlap those on discrimination on the basis of sex, religion, national origin, or age.

The Title VII prohibition is broad, embracing virtually all aspects of the employer-employee relationship. Guidance in determining what "compensation" includes may be obtained both from EEOC and court rulings and from interpretations issued under the Equal Pay Act by the Labor Department.

In an Interpretative Bulletin on Equal Pay for Equal Work, the Labor Department defines "wages" to include "all payments made to or on behalf of the employee as remuneration for employment"—straight time and overtime. (See FEP 401: 601, 611.)

Guidance in the interpretation of the broader category of "wages, hours and other terms and conditions of employment" may be found in refusal-to-bargain decisions under the Taft-Hartley Act.

The NLRB and the courts have construed the phrase to include a variety of subjects, including various fringe benefits—bonuses, company housing, employee stock-purchase plans, group insurance, lunch and rest periods, individual merit raises, and employee discounts. Discrimination involving any of these matters would come within the scope of Title VII.

In addition, the EEOC and the Labor Department's Office of Federal Contract Compliance Programs have decided that the duty not to discriminate extends to the physical environment in which

10

an employee works. So unequal treatment regarding such facilities as rest rooms, lunch rooms, and drinking fountains could be the basis for a charge of discrimination.

SEGREGATION, CLASSIFICATION

Under Title VII, it also is an unfair employment practice for an employer to limit, segregate, or classify employees in any way that would deprive or tend to deprive any individual of employment opportunities or otherwise adversely affect his status as an employee because of his race, color, religion, sex, or national origin.

Separate seniority rosters for male and female and white and black employees have been held to be violations of Title VII in such cases as Griggs v. Duke Power Co. and U.S. v. Jacksonville Terminal Co. (3 FEP Cases 175, 3 FEP Cases 862)

HIRING PRACTICES

Even before an individual is on an employer's payroll, he may charge unlawful discrimination under Title VII.

It is unlawful employment practice, for example, to indicate a preference, limitation, specification, or discrimination based on race, color, religion, sex, or national origin in printing or publishing any employment notices or advertising. The same is true with respect to age.

Title VII does not expressly ban preemployment inquiries as to race, color, religion, sex, or national origin. But taking a lead from state fair employment practice agencies, the EEOC has indicated it will disapprove such inquiries except where sex, religion, or national origin is a bona fide occupational qualification. (FEP Manual 401:61) The Age Discrimination in Employment Act discussed below permits an employer in an employment application to require an answer as to "date of birth" or "age" provided the question does not conceal a discriminatory purpose.

Unlawful Preemployment Questions. Guidelines on questions an employer may ask an applicant have been issued by a number of state agencies. Among the inquiries forbidden are:

► Change of name.
► Maiden or former name of spouse.
► Previous foreign addresses.
► Birthplace of applicant, applicant's spouse, parents, or relatives.

▶ Applicant's religion.

▶ Applicant's complexion or color of skin.

▶ Applicant's citizenship or national origin.

▶ Applicant's foreign military service, although an inquiry as to the applicant's service in the U.S. Armed Forces is permitted.

▶ Name and address of relative, not person, to be notified in an emergency.

▶ Applicant's membership in clubs or organizations except those that do not reveal applicant's color, race, national origin, religion, or sex.

▶ Applicant's arrest or conviction record. An arrest record was held not to be a valid basis for refusal to hire in Gregory v. Litton Systems, Inc. (5 FEP Cases 267) The same rule applies to a conviction record except where there is a business necessity, such as a case in which a person with a conviction record applies for a hotel job in which he would have access to guests' rooms and property. (See Green v. Missouri Pacific R.R. Co., 10 FEP Cases 1409; Richardson v. Hotel Corp. of America, 3 FEP Cases 1031.)

▶ An applicant's height except where it is a bona fide occupational qualification.

There are, however, a number of questions that generally may be asked an applicant. They include whether the applicant has worked under another name, what languages he speaks or reads, what is his educational record, what is his work experience, who are his character references, what U.S. military experience does he have, what is his place of residence, whether he is an alien, and, if so, does he have a right to remain in the United States to work, and whether his age exceeds the minimum required under child-labor laws.

Basic Policy. Whether particular hiring or promotion policies are discriminatory usually is determined by the test laid down by the Supreme Court in Griggs v. Duke Power Co. Under this test, if an action or policy, although neutral on its face, is discriminatory in effect, it is unlawful unless it is shown there is a substantial business justification for the policy. (3 FEP Cases 175) The Court also held in Griggs that a requirement that an applicant have a high school education must be sufficiently related to successful performance in the job involved to be lawful. Both the standard intelligence test given to applicants and the educational requirements were found by the Court in Duke Power to disqualify black applicants at a higher rate than white applicants and were not job-related. See below under "Seniority Systems" for decisions (Teamsters, United Air Lines) amplifying and qualifying the Griggs decision.

Other recruiting or hiring practices found by the courts or the EEOC to violate Title VII include:

▶ Word-of-mouth recruiting or recruiting at only predominately white institutions where there is an existing imbalance in the work force. (U.S. v. Georgia Power, 5 FEP Cases 587)

▶ Enforcement of grooming standards prohibiting "bush" hair styles and handlebar and Fu Manchu mustaches. (EEOC Decision No. 72-0979, Feb. 3, 1972; EEOC Decision No. 71-2444, June 10, 1971, 4 FEP Cases 18)

▶ Refusal to employ individuals because of their poor credit records. (EEOC Decision No. 72-0427, Aug. 31, 1971, 4 FEP Cases 304)

▶ Rejection of an applicant based on adverse personnel reports from other companies without giving the applicant an opportunity to rebut the reports. (EEOC Decision No. 72-0974, Feb. 2, 1972, 4 FEP Cases 1305; EEOC Decision No. 72-2103, June 27, 1972, 4 FEP Cases 1169)

▶ Preferential hiring of relatives of present employees where the present work force contains a disproportionately low percentage of minority-group workers. (EEOC Decision No. 71-797, 3 FEP Cases 266)

▶ A requirement for union membership and listing on an experience roster for job referrals which has the effect of excluding a greater proportion of women than men from available jobs. (Kaplan v. IATSE, 11 FEP Cases 872)

▶ Use of a minimum height requirement where it had the effect of excluding a substantially greater number of women and Spanish-surnamed Americans than Caucasian males. (EEOC Decision No. 71-1418, March 17, 1971, 3 FEP Cases 580)

▶ Denial of employment to unwed mothers in an area where blacks had a significantly higher rate of illegitimate births and where there was no showing of business necessity. (EEOC Decision No. 71-382, Oct. 30, 1970, 3 FEP Cases 230)

Business Necessity. Despite the indication by the Supreme Court in Griggs v. Duke Power that a policy that has a discriminatory impact might be justified on the ground of business necessity, the EEOC and the courts have construed the exception narrowly.

The Supreme Court itself, for example, has made it clear that "business necessity" does not encompass such matters as inconvenience, annoyance, or expense to the employer. The only permissible reason for tolerating a policy with a discriminatory impact, the Court said in Duke Power, is business necessity that is "related to job performance."

In other cases, federal courts of appeals have added these interpretations of business necessity as justification for policies that have a discriminatory effect:

► Necessity connotes an "irresistible demand." To be retained, the practice or policy "must not only directly foster safety and efficiency," but also must be essential to those goals. If those legitimate goals can be served by a reasonably available alternative system with less discriminatory effects, then the system may not be retained. The holding was by the Second Circuit Court of Appeals. (U.S. v. Bethlehem Steel Co., 3 FEP Cases 589)

► The test is "not merely whether there exists a business purpose for adhering to a challenged practice." Rather, "the test is whether the alleged purpose is so essential to the safe and efficient operation of the business as to override any racial impact." The decision was by the Fourth Circuit. (Robinson v. Lorillard Corp., 3 FEP Cases 653)

► An employer's burden of proof of a business necessity may vary depending on the nature of the job, the Tenth Circuit stated in upholding an airline's requirement of a college degree and 500 hours of flight time for the position of flight officer. When a job requires a small amount of skill and training, the courts scrutinize closely any preemployment standards or criteria that discriminate against minorities. The employer has a heavy burden to demonstrate that the criteria are job-related. But there is a correspondingly lighter burden where the job requires a high degree of skill, and the economic and human risks in hiring an unqualified applicant are great. (Spurlock v. United Airlines, 5 FEP Cases 17)

Quota or Goal Hiring. Section 703(j) of Title VII explicitly bars any interpretation that would accord preferential treatment to any individual or group because of race, color, or national origin because of an imbalance that may exist with respect to the total number or percentage of persons of such race, color, or national origin in any community, state, section, or other area, or in the available work force in any community, state, section, or other area.

But where the racial imbalance is the result of discriminatory practices in violation of Title VII, a court may order a preference that will require an employer to hire or a union to accept as members a specified percentage of minority-group persons. Such preference is usually described as establishing "goals," instead of "quotas."

In a case involving a local of the Steamfitters, for example, the Second Circuit upheld the right of a district court to achieve a goal of a certain percentage of black and Puerto Rican members where the district court found a pattern of long-continued and egregious racial discrimination that permeated the steamfitting industry and precluded qualified nonwhite applicants from gaining membership.

The appeals court remanded the case, however, for an explanation of how the lower court reached its percentage figure or a determination of whether a lower percentage is appropriate. (Rios v. Steamfitters, Local 638, 8 FEP Cases 239)

In a later case, the Second Circuit refused to approve a permanent order of a district court requiring New York correctional and civil service officials, following development of a new selection procedure for promotions, to promote at least one black or Hispanic employee for each three whites promoted until the percentage of blacks or Hispanic sergeants equals the combined percentage of black and Hispanic correction officers.

The order, the Court said, completely ignores the statutory requirements and constitutional purpose of the state civil service law. It constitutes court-imposed "reverse" discrimination without any exceptional or compelling governmental purpose.

The court, however, did approve an order providing interim relief authorizing state correctional and civil service officials to apply for permission to make interim promotions pending development of new selection procedures. The order directed that at least one of every four promotions be from the class of minority-group persons challenging the selection procedures. The case was Kirkland v. Department of Correctional Services. (11 FEP Cases 38)

Government Contracts. In an action brought under Executive Order 11246, the U.S. Court of Appeals for the Third Circuit held that a contractors' association lacked standing to challenge the legality under Title VII and the U.S. Constitution of the Labor Department's revised "Philadelphia Plan" requiring contractors on federal and federally assisted contracts to make good-faith efforts to meet certain percentage goals for minority-group employment.

The court decided that the plan did not violate Title VII, despite a contention that the contractors would have to discriminate against white persons to meet the goals. It merely required contractors to make good-faith efforts to fulfill their commitments to meet the goals set in the plan. (Contractors Association of Eastern Pa. v. Shultz, 2 FEP Cases 472)

According to the Fifth Circuit, the obligations imposed upon government contractors under the Executive Order cannot extend beyond those imposed by Title VII with respect to seniority plans. If a seniority system is bona fide under Title VII, the Executive Order cannot be interpreted to require the employer to deviate from that system. (U.S. v. East Texas Motor Freight System, CA 5, 1977, 16 FEP Cases 163)

EMPLOYMENT TESTING

Under Title VII, it is not unlawful "for an employer to give and to act upon the results of any professionally developed ability test provided that such test, its administration or action upon the results is not designed, intended, or used to discriminate because of race, color, religion, sex, or national origin."

In 1966 and again in 1970, EEOC promulgated testing guidelines "to serve as a workable set of standards for employers, unions and employment agencies in determining whether their selection procedures conform with the obligations contained in Title VII." The guidelines applied to "any paper-and-pencil or performance measure used as a basis for any employment decision"—such as hiring, transfer, promotion, membership, training, referral, or retention. Any such measures or procedures which adversely affect those protected by Title VII constitute discrimination, EEOC said, "unless: (a) the test has been validated and evidences a high degree of utility . . . and (b) the person giving or acting upon the results of the particular test can demonstrate that alternative suitable hiring, transfer or promotion procedures are unavailable. . . ."

The standards EEOC laid out for validating tests—proving their job-relatedness—were very difficult to meet. Many industrial psychologists said the requirements went far beyond what the profession could achieve.

The result of the first few years of EEOC's "hard line" was that many employers abandoned testing programs entirely. As it became evident that the rules applied also to interviews and other procedures, many of which were subjective and even more difficult to justify, the pendulum began to swing back toward job-related tests and efforts—sometimes very expensive—to validate them.

Supreme Court Rulings: The Supreme Court has issued two

opinions having to do with EEOC's view of employment testing. In Griggs v. Duke Power Co., decided in 1971, the Court upheld EEOC's position that any test having an adverse effect on women or minority-group applicants must be job-related, regardless of whether the employer intended to discriminate. (3 FEP Cases 175) In Albemarle Paper Co. v. Moody, the Court said the EEOC selection guidelines are entitled to "great deference." (10 FEP Cases 1181) But early in 1978, in U.S. v. South Carolina, the Court (without issuing an opinion) upheld accepted professional standards where they were in conflict with the EEOC guidelines. (16 FEP Cases 501)

Development of Guidelines: The OFCCP concerns itself with testing and selection in its administration of Executive Order 11246 forbidding discrimination by federal contractors. Its testing regulations, first issued in 1968 and amended in 1971, differed somewhat from the EEOC standards. In addition, the U.S. Civil Service Commission issued its own considerably different standards for selection by public employers. An effort to combine all the varied standards into one set of uniform federal guidelines for employee selection procedures began in 1972.

Civil Service and the Departments of Labor and Justice promulgated a new set of Federal Executive Agency Guidelines in November 1976, but the two other agencies decided these new rules were not stringent enough. EEOC reissued its 1970 guidelines, taking the position that they provided stronger protection for minority groups and women. This left employers subject to two conflicting sets of government rules on the subject.

The Carter Administration revived the effort toward uniformity in 1977, and the result was a set of Uniform Guidelines on Employee Selection Procedures, proposed in December 1977 by EEOC, Civil Service, and the Departments of Justice and Labor. As this volume went to press, knowledgeable observers were predicting the uniform guidelines would be issued within a few months, in form very much like that proposed.

All the federal guidelines agree on requiring employers to validate tests and other procedures that result in adverse impact on minorities and women. The uniform guidelines use a four-fifths rule of thumb for guidance as to what adverse impact is significant: "A selection rate for any racial, ethnic or sex group which is less than four-fifths (4/5) (or 80 percent) of the rate for the group with the highest rate will generally be regarded . . . as evidence of adverse impact."

On the question of whether each step in a selection procedure must be studied for adverse impact, or whether employers should be judged on the overall results (the "bottom line"), the proposed guidelines have this to say: "If . . . the total selection process for a job has no adverse impact, the federal enforcement agencies . . . generally will not take enforcement action based upon adverse impact of any component of that process. . . ."

Three Methods of Validation: Testing specialists have used three methods of validating tests to make sure they are job-related. A test may be validated:

▶ By conducting a study to determine if those who do well on the test also do well on the job, and if those who do poorly on the test do poorly on the job. This is called "criterion-related validity."

▶ By determining that it is a representative sample of important or critical job behaviors, such as a typing test used to hire a typist. This is called "content validity."

▶ By showing that it measures the degree to which candidates have identifiable characteristics which have been determined to be important for successful job performance, such as a test for emotional stability used to hire a police officer. This is called "construct validity."

Where EEOC insisted on criterion-related validity studies unless they were not technically feasible, the FEA guidelines and the newly proposed uniform guidelines allow all three methods. The restrictions on construct validity in the new uniform guidelines, however, make it unlikely to be a useful strategy, according to many industrial psychologists.

Those demonstrating job-relatedness through criterion-related validity studies are obligated to perform such studies for each group taking the test, to make sure it is equally predictive of job performance for members of each group. Test users are subject to this requirement unless it is not technically feasible to perform such studies. This concept of "differential validity," found in all the federal guidelines, is a discredited idea so far as the psychological profession is concerned, according to representatives of professional organizations. Nonetheless, it remains a requirement.

The new guidelines encourage cooperative efforts at test validation, and test users are permitted to use validity evidence developed elsewhere if job analyses show the jobs to be the same and certain other conditions are met.

EMPLOYMENT CONDITIONS

The prohibitions on discrimination with respect to employment conditions are extremely broad. The Title VII prohibition, for example, extends to discrimination relating to "compensation, terms, conditions, or privileges of employment."

The executive order applicable to government contractors requires affirmative action to provide equal employment opportunity in "employment, upgrading, demotion or transfer, recruitment or recruitment advertising, layoff or termination, rates of pay or other forms of compensation, and selection for training, including apprenticeship."

There are many examples in which employment conditions may result in disparate treatment on the basis of race or national origin and so violate Title VII. Some are:

► Paying Caucasian employees average higher bonuses than black employees where the employer's stated reason for the disparity would not withstand scrutiny. (EEOC Sixth Annual Report)

► Applying safety rules disparately where it was shown that race was a factor in the administration of the rules. (EEOC Decision, April 22, 1976, Case No. 71-1885, 3 FEP Cases 1025)

► Assignment of crews on an all-white or all-black basis, with no evidence to show the basis of the assignments. Providing better housing for whites than blacks. (EEOC decision, Nov. 11, 1970, Case No. 71-453, 3 FEP Cases 384)

► Maintaining an informal, inadequate training program that discouraged blacks from bidding on and receiving assistance in traditionally all-white job classifications. (EEOC Decision, July 24, 1969, Case 68-112E, 2 FEP Cases 168)

► Banning the use of Spanish during working as well as non-working time where there was no showing that it was necessary for supervisors to understand all conversations among the Spanish-surnamed employees. (EEOC Sixth Annual Report)

► Discharging an employee because his or her wages were garnished twice within a 12-month period. (Wallace v. Debron Corp., 7 FEP Cases 595)

▶ Maintaining a working atmosphere in which racial insults were permitted. (EEOC Sixth Annual Report)

▶ Enforcing standards of grooming and appearance "without regard to racially different physiological and cultural characteristics." (EEOC Decision, June 10, 1971, Decision No. 71-2444, 4 FEP Cases 18)

SENIORITY SYSTEMS

The principal issue regarding seniority is the impact of Title VII on establishing seniority systems that may perpetuate the effects of pre-Act or post-Act discrimination. Does the Section 703(h) exemption for bona fide seniority systems insulate them against discrimination charges, even though the system may be discriminatory in effect? It does, the courts have said, so long as the system isn't a guise for unlawful discrimination.

During its 1976-77 Term, the Supreme Court handed down some landmark decisions on the interplay between Title VII and contractual seniority systems.

The first decision by the Supreme Court on the seniority issue involved black truck drivers who were hired only for city-driving jobs. There also was a discriminatory transfer policy under which blacks were not permitted to transfer to over-the-road driving jobs.

Finding that the blacks discriminatorily had been denied over-the-road jobs, the Court decided that retroactive seniority back to the date of application was an appropriate remedy—one that would put the black drivers in their "rightful places." Such relief may be denied, the Court added, only on the basis of "unusual" and adverse impact on other employees. (Franks v. Bowman Transportation Co., 12 FEP Cases 549)

Then in 1977, the Supreme Court added some significant qualifications to the doctrine. The case, Teamsters v. U.S., was similar to the Bowman case. The company had refused to hire blacks and Spanish-surnamed employees for over-the-road driving jobs.

Members of the minority groups were hired only for city-driving jobs, and separate seniority rosters were maintained. A city-driver hired for an over-the-road job forfeited his accumulated seniority and started at the bottom of the list for over-the-road seniority.

The discriminatory hiring practices were reinforced by a discriminatory transfer policy. Only white city-drivers were permitted to transfer to over-the-road jobs. Both the hiring and transfer policies were not discontinued until a suit was brought by the Justice Department.

The key to the Supreme Court's decision was the Section 703(h) exemption for bona fide seniority systems. A seniority system that is adopted without a discriminatory motive, the Court said, is insulated from attack by Section 703(h).

The fact that the seniority system perpetuated pre-Act discrimination, even post-Act discrimination, the Court said, does not affect its bona fide status. Section 703(h) immunizes all bona fide seniority systems. It does not distinguish between the perpetuation of pre-Act discrimination and post-Act discrimination.

The decision makes some far-reaching changes in the interpretation of Title VII as applied by the courts below. Here are the principal changes:

► What had been treated as departmental seniority must be treated under the Teamsters case as hiring and transfer discrimination. A number of lower court decisions had required employers and unions to replace departmental or craft seniority with plant-wide seniority.

► To obtain financial or seniority relief, the plaintiffs must establish that they were subject to post-Act hiring or transfer discrimination. Lower court decisions prior to the Supreme Court's decision had awarded plaintiffs back pay, preferential transfer and promotion, and adjustment of seniority where it was found that an employer and a union had maintained a seniority policy that perpetuated any prior discrimination unless compelled by business necessity.

► Statistics showing a racial imbalance in the composition of the employer's work force as compared with the composition of the population in the surrounding community may be used to establish a prima facie case of racial discrimination. But such statistics are not irrefutable, and, like any other kind of evidence, they may be rebutted. (Teamsters v. U.S. [T.I.M.E.–D.C., Inc.], 14 FEP Cases 1514)

The Teamsters decision dealt only with the seniority system. In a case decided the same day, the Court added a new point to the doctrine. An airline discharged a stewardess in 1968 pursuant to its policy of not employing married stewardesses. The policy was abandoned in 1972, and the stewardess was rehired.

In 1973, more than one year later, she filed a charge with the EEOC, alleging that the company's policy of refusing to credit prior service for seniority was unlawful as perpetuating prior discrimination. The Court rejected the claim on two grounds.

► First, it said the seniority system, which based seniority solely on current employment, was bona fide and so protected by Section 703(h).

► Second, the Court pointed out that the charge was not filed within 90 days (the time limit was raised to 180 days in 1972). So the Court decided the case should be dismissed. (United Airlines v. Evans, 14 FEP Cases 1510)

Under the reasoning of these two cases, the plaintiff must show:

► The employer maintained a discriminatory hiring or transfer policy after the effective date of the Act (July 1, 1965).

► The plaintiff applied for and was denied a job in the all-white, all-male category after the effective date of the Act or established that it would have been futile because of the employer's known discriminatory policy.

► The plaintiff challenged the denial of his application by filing a charge with the EEOC within the 90-day or 180-day time limit.

In a 1978 decision, the Supreme Court added to the rules for establishing and rebutting a charge of discrimination. In rebutting a prima facie case of Title VII racial discrimination, the Court said, the employer must prove that its employment procedures are based on legitimate considerations. But it need not prove that these procedures allow consideration of the largest number of minority applicants.

The Court added that an employer's proof that its work force was racially balanced or that the work force contained a disproportionately high percentage of minority employees is relevant, for purposes of rebutting a prima facie case, to the issue of whether an unexplained rejection of minority applicants was discriminatorily motivated. Such proof, however, cannot conclusively resolve the issue. (Furnco Construction Corp. v. Waters, 17 FEP Cases 1062)

APPLICATION OF TIME LIMIT TO EEOC

In a later decision, however, the Supreme Court held that the EEOC is not required to bring an action in court within 180 days of the filing of a charge. The statute of limitations *was not* perceived in terms of a limitation on the EEOC's right to sue.

Moreover, the Court added, Title VII actions brought by the EEOC are not subject to state statutes of limitations. So it was held that the EEOC could maintain an action that it brought approximately three years and two months after the charge was filed and five months after conciliation efforts had failed, even though the analagous state limitation period was one year. (Occidental Life Ins. Co. v. EEOC, 14 FEP Cases 1718)

Suits brought under the 1866 Act (42 U.S.C. Sec. 1981) are not subject to any federal statute of limitations. The courts apply the appropriate state statute.

'LAST HIRED, FIRST FIRED'

In addition to the Supreme Court decisions on seniority, there have been a number of decisions by circuit courts of appeals. Many of these cases involved layoff, and the plaintiffs sought earlier seniority dates to avoid layoff.

Four courts of appeals have upheld "last-hired, first-fired" plant-wide or company-wide seniority systems as bona fide under Title VII.

The Seventh Circuit did so in Waters v. Wisconsin Steel Works, the Third Circuit in Jersey Central Power & Light Co. v. IBEW, the Fifth Circuit in Watkins v. Steelworkers, and the Second Circuit in Chance v. Board of Examiners. (8 FEP Cases 577, 9 FEP Cases 117, 10 FEP Cases 1297, 11 FEP Cases 1450)

In finding the seniority system to be bona fide in the Waters case, the court noted that the discrimination perpetuated by the seniority system was a refusal to hire that continued until the date Title VII was enacted. But in upholding the seniority system, the court said that "Title VII speaks only to the future."

Both Title VII and the 1866 Act (42 U.S.C. Sec. 1981) were involved in the Watkins case. Reversing a district court decision, the circuit court held that the company did not violate either law by using a long-established seniority system for determining who would be laid off and rehired, even though it resulted in the discharge of more blacks than whites to the point of eliminating blacks from the work force. In support of its holding, the court noted:

► The present hiring policy is nondiscriminatory and has been for over ten years.

▶ The seniority system was adopted without intent to discriminate.

▶ The individuals laid off under the system were not themselves the subjects of prior employment discrimination.

In the Chance case, the U.S. Court of Appeals for the Second Circuit upheld a "last hired, first fired" policy for the layoff of supervisors in a school system in a case brought under the Civil Rights Acts of 1866 and 1871. The court, rejecting the district court's imposition of a quota system for layoffs, reasoned that, "if racial quotas prevent the excessing (layoff) of a black or Puerto Rican, a white person with greater seniority must be excessed in his place." The result would be "constitutionally forbidden reverse discrimination." (11 FEP Cases 1450)

In a case involving a somewhat different aspect of seniority and layoff, the U.S. Court of Appeals for the Second Circuit reversed and remanded a district court decision that denied relief to female police officers who were laid off on the basis of seniority.

In remanding the case, the circuit court said that neither Section 703(h) (bona fide seniority systems) nor Section 703(j) (preferential treatment) precludes relief where the officer might prove that she would have been hired sooner than she actually was in the absence of discrimination by demonstrating:

▶ That she actually filed an application for employment or wrote a letter complaining about the discriminatory hiring policy early enough during the period of discrimination;

▶ That she had expressed a desire to enlist in the police force, but was deterred by a discriminatory practice barring women. (Acha v. Beame, 12 FEP Cases 257)

Upon remand, the district court held that the police department violated Title VII by laying off the female police officers who, but for their sex, would have been hired early enough to accumulate sufficient seniority to withstand layoff. (Acha v. Beame, 13 FEP Cases 17)

▶ Upon reconsideration in the light of the Supreme Court's rulings in the Teamsters and United Airlines cases, the district court held that the discriminatees were limited to a revised seniority date of no earlier than March 24, 1972—the date of extension of Title VII to municipal employees. (Acha v. Beame, 15 FEP Cases 414)

SEX DISCRIMINATION

The ban on employment discrimination based on sex was inserted during the debate on the floor of the House. So there was little legislative history to clarify the congressional intent.

As a result, the EEOC and the courts have had difficulty in applying the sex prohibition. In revised Guidelines on Discrimination Because of Sex published in 1972 (FEP 401:29), the EEOC made these major points:

► It is an unlawful employment practice to classify a job as "male" or "female" or to maintain separate lines of progression or separate seniority lines based on sex, where this would adversely affect any employee, unless sex is a bona fide occupational qualification for the job.

► Advertising in "male" and "female" help-wanted columns is unlawful, unless sex is a bona fide occupational qualification.

► State "protective" laws for women that limit employment in certain occupations, such as those requiring lifting objects exceeding specified weights, working during certain hours of the night, working for more than a specified number of hours in a day or a week or for certain periods of time before and after childbirth, conflict with and are superseded by Title VII. (FEP 431:35) So such laws will not be considered a defense to an otherwise established unlawful employment practice or a basis for application of the bona fide occupational qualification exception.

► Rules that limit or restrict the employment of married women and are not applicable to married men amount to discrimination based on sex in violation of Title VII.

► Discrimination between men and women in payment of "fringe benefits" is unlawful. This includes such benefits as medical, hospital, life insurance, retirement, profit-sharing, and bonuses. Moreover, the EEOC has stated that conditioning benefits available to employees and their spouses on whether the employee is the

25

"head of the household" or "principal wage earner" will be found a prima facie violation of Title VII, since such status has no relationship to job performance.

▶ EEOC also has said that it is unlawful for an employer to make available benefits for the wives and families of male employees where the same benefits are not made to the husbands and families of female employees; it also is considered unlawful to make available benefits for the wives of male employees that are not made available to female employees, or to make available benefits for the husbands of female employees that are not available to male employees.

▶ An employment policy that excludes from employment applicants or employees because of pregnancy is considered in prima facie violation of Title VII.

▶ A refusal to hire because of the preferences of co-workers, the employer, clients, or customers (except where it is necessary for the purposes of authenticity or genuineness, such as the preference to have actresses play women's parts in plays or movies).

WORKING MOTHERS

The first Supreme Court decision involving alleged discrimination based on sex tested a company rule against hiring women with pre-school age children where there was no such rule for men.

The Court said that the test of whether a bona fide occupational qualification exists is whether it can be shown that the qualification is "demonstrably more relevant to job performances for a woman than for a man." The case involved Martin Marietta Corp., and the Supreme Court vacated the judgment below and remanded the case for further findings on the stated issue. (3 FEP Cases 40)

In a related case involving the refusal of Southern Bell Telephone Co. to employ women as telephone "switchmen" because of asserted "strenuous" lifting involved, the Fifth Circuit made this ruling: The test of whether a BFOQ exists is whether there is reasonable cause to believe that all or substantially all women would be unable to perform the duties of the job involved safely and efficiently.

The company argued that few women safely could life 30 pounds, while all men could. The court found that the company did not meet its burden of proof, stating that the company may not impose its own weight limit for lifting by women. (1 FEP Cases 656)

STATE PROTECTIVE LAWS

Early in the century, many states enacted laws intended to protect women from hazards of industrial life by restricting the hours they might work, the weights they might lift, and the jobs they might fill.

After Title VII was adopted, the idea was pressed that these laws, instead of helping women, might restrict their job opportunities. A law limiting the hours a woman may work to eight hours a day, for example, could pose an obstacle to employment in executive jobs requiring work in excess of eight hours a day.

In its guidelines, the EEOC has taken the position that such laws and regulations conflict with Title VII and may not be the basis for a defense to a charge of unlawful discrimination based on sex. (FEP 401:29) A number of federal courts have supported this view. (See FEP 451:i.)

A different type of law requires that certain benefits be given to women, such as minimum wages, premium pay for overtime, rest periods, or physical facilities. The EEOC has taken the position that such laws do not provide a defense to a refusal to hire a woman because the employer does not wish to take on the expense of complying with the state law. It also takes the position that such requirements do not discriminate against men, since the employer may provide the same benefits for men, unless the employer can prove that business necessity precludes providing such benefits for both women and men. Upon a showing of business necessity, the state law would be found to conflict with Title VII and would be superseded.

In the Potlatch Forests case, for example, the Eighth Circuit found that a state law requiring employers to pay premium rates to women does not conflict with Title VII. The conflict may be resolved, the court said, by paying men the same premium overtime rates. (4 FEP Cases 1037) The Ninth Circuit, however, held the other way in the Homemakers, Inc., case. It said that, although EEOC guidelines are entitled to great deference, this is not so where they call for modifications in substantive state law. (10 FEP Cases 633)

Later interpreting its Southern Bell decision, the Fifth Circuit held in Long v. Sapp that it could find no "factual basis for believing that all or substantially all women would be unable to perform" the job of "warehousemen" where co-workers expressed doubt that any woman could do the work involved. In explanation, the court said that "although a more objective evaluation might bear the workers out, their subjective doubts, which may themselves be based on impermissible stereotypes, are no substitute for the objective evidence" demanded by the women suing Southern Bell. (8 FEP Cases 1079)

FLIGHT ATTENDANTS

For many years, most U.S. airlines limited the jobs of flight attendants to unmarried women. This has been changed as a result of litigation under Title VII. (See "Seniority Systems," pp. 20-22, for discussion of another aspect of this problem.)

In a case decided in 1971, the Fifth Circuit rejected a Pan American Airways argument that sex (woman) is a BFOQ for the position of flight cabin attendant. The court said the test is whether "the essence of the business operation would be undermined by not hiring members of one sex exclusively."

The court continued that the employer must show not only that it is impractical to find men with requisite abilities, but also that the abilities are necessary and not merely tangential. So an airline may not exclude all males from the position simply because most males would be unable to perform adequately. (3 FEP Cases 469)

In later cases involving United, Northwest, and Continental Airlines, the Fifth and Seventh Circuits and some district courts found there was no BFOQ in a rule requiring stewardesses, but not stewards, to be unmarried. In the United Air Lines case, the court said: "The marital status of a stewardess cannot be said to affect the individual women's ability to create the proper psychological climate of comfort, safety, and security of passengers. Nor does any passenger preference for single stewardesses provide a basis for invoking the rule." (3 FEP Cases 621, 8 FEP Cases 659, 7 FEP Cases 687, 8 FEP Cases 1237) But where only women held positions as flight attendants, so that they were not competing with married males, the Fifth Circuit found no sex discrimination in a no-marriage rule. (Stroud v. Delta Air Lines, 14 FEP Cases 206)

A number of other types of disparate treatment of male and female cabin attendants have been held to violate Title VII in such cases as those involving Northwest and Continental Airlines. The unlawful practices included:

▶ Paying lower salaries or pensions to stewardesses than those paid to male pursers.

► Requiring stewardesses to share double rooms during layovers, while providing male pursers with single rooms.

► Providing male pursers with a cleaning allowance for uniforms, while not providing such an allowance for stewardesses.

► Requiring stewardesses, but not male cabin attendants, to comply with weight restrictions.

► Forbidding stewardesses, but not male cabin attendants, to wear glasses.

► Imposing shorter maximum-height requirements on stewardesses than on male cabin attendants.

► Limiting stewardesses, but not male cabin attendants, in their choice of luggage to be carried onto planes.

► Imposing chain of command aboard planes under which all male cabin attendants, regardless of classification or length of service, are superior to all female flight attendants.

► Discriminating on the basis of sex in filling cabin attendants' positions unless sex constitutes a BFOQ. (7 FEP Cases 687, 8 FEP Cases 1237)

Note, however, that some courts have held that weight or height standards, like hair-length rules, may be applied differently to males and females without violating Title VII. (4 FEP Cases 799, 1767 1802)

MATERNITY LEAVE

In two cases decided in 1974, the Supreme Court held that school boards violated the Due Process Clause of the Fourteenth Amendment to the Constitution by requiring school teachers to take maternity leave without pay or to quit their jobs after a specified period of pregnancy. The cases involved the Cleveland and Chesterfield County School Boards. (6 FEP Cases 1253)

PREGNANCY AS DISABILITY

Another issue involving pregnancy is whether it is an illness or a disability for the purpose of state disability insurance laws or collective bargaining contracts.

The first case to reach the Supreme Court involved the California disability insurance program. The Court decided that the State's policy of not providing disability benefits for women unable to work because of normal pregnancy does not violate the Equal

Protection of the Laws Clause of the Constitution. The case was Geduldig v. Aiello. (8 FEP Cases 97) The Court, however, did not decide whether the denial of compensation for losses caused by pregnancy would violate Title VII of the Civil Rights Act.

Subsequently, the Supreme Court struck down a Utah statute that made pregnant women ineligible for unemployment compensation for a period beginning 12 weeks before the expected date of childbirth and ending six weeks after childbirth. This law, the Court said, violated the Due Process Clause of the Constitution. The case was Turner v. Department of Employment Security. (11 FEP Cases 721)

But the most significant decision was handed down in late 1976 in Gilbert v. General Electric Co.—a class action involving an estimated 100,000 claimants. The issue was whether the company violated Title VII by excluding "disability" due to pregnancy from its employee disability benefits plan. The Fourth Circuit held that the exclusion was a violation of Title VII. (10 FEP Cases 1201) Similar holdings were handed down by the Second and Third Circuits in cases involving American Telephone & Telegraph Co. and Liberty Mutual Insurance Co. (10 FEP Cases 435, 9 FEP Cases 227)

The Supreme Court reversed the General Electric holding. By a six-to-three margin, the Court held that the exclusion of pregnancy disability from the disability benefits plan did not violate Title VII. It refused to follow the EEOC's guideline that would require an employer to treat disability due to pregnancy as a temporary disability under any health or temporary disability insurance or sick-leave plan available in connection with employment. (13 FEP Cases 1657) Later, the Supreme Court held in the Nashville Gas case that denial of sick-leave pay to pregnant employees was not a *per se* violation of Title VII, but that denial of accumulated seniority upon return from pregnancy was a violation. (16 FEP Cases 146)

NEWSPAPER ADVERTISING

Any sex-oriented advertising to fill job openings is considered a violation of Title VII by the EEOC. An ad may not designate sex either expressly or impliedly as a condition for employment unless sex is a bona fide occupational qualification for the position.

In the first landmark decision in this area, the Supreme Court held that a newspaper's free-speech rights were not infringed by an order of the Pittsburgh Human Relations Commission forbidding the carrying of help-wanted advertisement in sex-designated columns. The case involved the Pittsburgh Press Co. (5 FEP Cases 1141)

But in another case, Brush v. Newspaper Publishing Co., the Ninth Circuit held that a newspaper publishing "male-female" jobs is not an "employment agency" within the meaning of Title VII. So it is not a violation, the Court said, for a newspaper to publish help-wanted ads expressing a preference as to sex. The Supreme Court denied review of the holding. (5 FEP Cases 20, 587)

DISCRIMINATION AGAINST MEN

Most sex discrimation cases have involved women. But there have been some cases in which men were denied employment in certain jobs and sex was found not to be a bona fide occupational qualification.

In a 1971 case, for example, the Fifth Circuit held that Pan American Airways violated Title VII by refusing to hire a man as a cabin flight attendant. The primary function of an airline, the court said, is to transport passengers safely, and no one has suggested that having male stewards seriously will affect this function. (3 FEP Cases 337)

Another way an employer can discriminate against a man is by taking his draft status into account in deciding whether to hire. But all circumstances must be considered. If, for example, a man is scheduled to enter the service in two weeks, an employer may take this into account in deciding whether to hire him. (EEOC Case No. 7067, July 31, 1969, 2 FEP Cases 167)

INSURANCE, PENSION BENEFITS

Prior to the adoption of Title VII, many companies had retirement plans that contained different compulsory or optional retirement ages for men and women. This also was the practice under the Social Security Act, which made a distinction between a normal retirement age of 62 for women and 65 for men.

But EEOC has ruled that when a pension plan differentiates between the sexes either in standard (such as age of eligibility for a pension) or benefits for survivors there is a violation of Title VII. This position has been upheld by courts in such cases as Bartmess

v. Drewrys U.S.A., Inc. (3 FEP Cases 795), Fitzpatrick v. Bitzer (8 FEP Cases 875, aff'd, US SupCt, 12 FEP Cases 1586), and Chastang v. Flynn and Emrich Co. (12 FEP Cases 1533).

The same principle has been applied by the EEOC to the vesting of contributions to profit-sharing plans. Different vesting rules for men and women are considered by the EEOC to be a violation of Title VII.

So under the rules applied by the EEOC all aspects of an insurance, retirement, profit-sharing, or other fringe-benefit plan must be equal without regard to sex.

But the Wage-Hour Division in the Labor Department has taken a different view where an employer makes contributions to or pays in full the cost of an insurance or pension plan for the employees.

Since employer contributions to such a plan are considered "wages" under the Equal Pay Act, the Division takes the position that the plan will be lawful if it meets one of these two tests:

► The employer's contributions to the plan are equal for men and women performing equal work; or

► The benefits under the plan are equal for men and women performing equal work. (See FEP 421:307.)

In the first decision involving pension plan contributions and Title VII, the Supreme Court appeared to move in the direction of EEOC's position. The case involved a contributory retirement, disability, and death benefit program. The monthly benefits for men and women of the same age, seniority, and salary were equal. Based on a study of mortality tables and its own experience, the employer determined that its women employees, on the average, live longer than the men employees. So it required the women to make contributions to the fund that were 14.8 percent higher than those required of the men. Since the contributions were withheld from pay checks, a woman took home less pay than a man earning the same salary. The plan later was amended so that there was no distinction, either in contributions or benefits, between the sexes.

The Supreme Court decided that the requirement that women make higher contributions than men was unlawful discrimination based on sex under Title VII. It rejected contentions that (1) the differential in take-home pay because of the higher contributions made by women was offset by the difference in pension benefits provided to the two classes of employees, and (2) the differential was based on a factor "other than sex" and so protected under the

Bennett Amendment to Title VII. The Court distinguished the case from the General Electric case on disability benefits for pregnancy. The pension program, it said, discriminated on the basis of sex, whereas the pregnancy plan discriminated on the basis of a special physical disability.

The Court, however, denied retroactive back pay in the pension case, and it raised a question about a broad application of the holding by stating:

"Nothing in our holding implies that it would be unlawful for an employer to set aside equal retirement contributions for each employee and let each retiree purchase the largest benefit which his or her contributions could command in the open market. Nor does it call in question the insurance company practice of considering the composition of the employer's work-force in determining the probable cost of a retirement or death benefit plan." (City of Los Angeles v. Manhart, 17 FEP Cases 395)

GROOMING STANDARDS

A number of employers apply different standards on hair length to men and women. Most of the appellate courts have held that refusing to hire or discharging men because of hair length is not unlawful sex discrimination.

In a case involving the Macon-Telegraph Publishing Co., the Fifth Circuit said that a hiring policy that distinguishes between men and women on the basis of a grooming policy is related more closely to an employer's choice of how to run its business than to equality of employment opportunity. The distinction, the court added, is based upon something other than immutable or protected characteristics. (9 FEP Cases 189)

The District of Columbia Circuit said that an employer may maintain reasonable good-grooming regulations because the image of the employer created by its employees dealing with the public on company assignments affects its relations with the public. The employer was the National Cash Register Company. (5 FEP Cases 1335)

In deciding that imposing different grooming standards for men and women does not violate Title VII, the Ninth Circuit reasoned that Title VII refers to unfair employment practices directed against individuals as a class simply because of their sex. Hair length standards are not directed against a class because of sex.

The case involved the California Land Title Co. (8 FEP Cases 1313)

The Eighth Circuit followed the same line of reasoning in a case involving the Missouri Pacific Railroad Co. Because the policies were reasonable and applied even-handedly, the court said, slight differences in appearance requirements for men and women had only a negligible effect on employment opportunities. (11 FEP Cases 1231)

For other cases deciding the same way, see Knott v. Missouri Pacific Railroad Co., CA 8 (1975), 11 FEP Cases 1231; Long v. Carlisle DeCoppet & Co., CA 2 (1976), 12 FEP Cases 1668; Earwood v. Continental Southeastern Line, CA 4 (1976), 14 FEP Cases 694; and Barker v. Taft Broadcasting Co., CA 6 (1977), 14 FEP Cases 697.

'REVERSE' DISCRIMINATION

Title VII makes it an unfair employment practice for an employer to discriminate in any aspect of the employment relationship on the basis of race, color, religion, sex, or national origin.

The 1866 Act, 42 U.S.C. Sec. 1981, gives all persons the same right to make and enforce contracts "as is enjoyed by white citizens."

But Section 703(j) of Title VII established an important exception to the discrimination prohibition. Called the "quota" provision, this section states that nothing in the title should be interpreted to require an employer, an employment agency, a union or a hiring hall, to grant preferential treatment to any individual or to any group because of the race, color, religion, sex, or national origin of such individual or group "on account of an imbalance which may exist" in such employment as compared with the total or percentage of such persons "in any community, state, section, or other area, or in the available work force in any community, state, section or other area."

This section has raised a number of questions and has resulted in important litigation. Among the questions presented:

► Does Title VII apply equally to discrimination against blacks and whites?

► Does the 1866 Act apply to discrimination against whites?

► Does Title VII apply equally to discrimination against women and men?

► Does an affirmative action plan that requires an employer to establish goals to obtain and maintain certain percentages of women and minority-group members on the payroll violate Title VII?

► Does a conciliation agreement that requires employers to give preference to women and minority-group members in hiring and promotion violate Title VII?

35

► How do the Due Process and Equal Protection of the Laws Clauses of the Constitution apply in such situations?

The Supreme Court gave an answer to the first two questions in the Sante Fe Trail Transportation case decided in 1976. It said that the prohibition against employment discrimination under both Title VII and the Act of 1866 applies to whites as well as blacks. Racial discrimination against whites is prohibited under Title VII under the same standard applied to blacks. Moreover, the Court added, the protection under the Act of 1866 applies to "all persons" and the phrase "as is enjoyed by white citizens" merely emphasizes the racial character of the rights protected. The Supreme Court rejected the holding of the court below that the 1866 Act did not protect whites. (12 FEP Cases 1577)

Answers to some of the other questions were provided by the Supreme Court in two cases disposed of in 1978. One case arose under Title VI of the Civil Rights Act of 1964; the other arose under Title VII and Executive Order 11246 applicable to government contractors. The results in the two cases were as follows:

► In the first case, the Court held that the medical school of the University of California at Davis violated Title VI of the Civil Rights Act of 1964 by maintaining a special admissions program that totally excluded nonminority group applicants from 16 percent of the seats in an entering class. Title VI forbids racial discrimination in any program or activity receiving federal financial assistance. But the Court went on to hold that the school may establish an admissions program involving "competitive consideration" of race and ethnic origin. The holding was by a five-to-four margin, and there was no majority opinion. (Regents of the University of California v. Bakke, 17 FEP Cases 1000) Although the decision was in an education, rather than employment, context, there was language suggesting that it could be translated to the employment area, and many attorneys in the field so construed it.

► In the second case, the Court refused to review the legality of a 1973 consent decree covering some 700,000 employees of the American Telephone & Telegraph Company and its subsidiaries. Three unions representing AT&T employees had urged the court to review the provisions of the decree that provide a promotional preference for classes of women, blacks, and other minorities, who were not themselves the specific victims of discrimination. The unions objected to seniority "override" provisions that abrogate seniority rights under their collective bargaining agreements. The Court's hands-off attitude was viewed by some as evidencing a tolerance toward preferential treatment for minority groups that had not themselves been discriminated against. (Communications Workers v. EEOC; Alliance of Independent Telephone Unions v. EEOC; 17 FEP Cases 1095)

Prior to the Supreme Court's Bakke decision, the Fifth Circuit held that a company and a union violated Title VII by implementing an affirmative action quota system under which black employees were given preference over senior white employees for admission to certain craft training programs. The court observed that the quota system improperly favored blacks who had not been the subject of prior unlawful discrimination and who already were in their "rightful place." (Weber v. Kaiser Aluminum Co., 16 FEP Cases 1)

This would appear contrary to the action taken by the Third Circuit in approving the consent decree in the AT&T case (above). The consent decree provided for goals, intermediate targets, and an "affirmative action override," even though it might benefit groups not shown to have been previously subjected to discrimination. (EEOC v. American Telephone & Telegraph Co., 14 FEP Cases 1210)

In earlier cases involving the Lathers and the Iron Workers, the Second Circuit made this statement: "While quotas merely to attain racial balance are forbidden, quotas to correct past discriminatory practices are not." (5 FEP Cases 318, 3 FEP Cases 496) In a case involving the Steamfitters, it set a membership goal of minority-group persons where the union had discriminated against blacks and Puerto Ricans. (8 FEP Cases 293)

Although clarification still is needed, it would appear that while fixed or rigid quotas would violate both Title VII and the Equal Protection Clause of the Constitution, there still is some leeway for giving special consideration to minority-group workers. Race may be used as one factor, among many, in making selections.

DISCRIMINATION AGAINST HOMOSEXUALS

Title VII does not specifically mention sexual preference as an unlawful basis of discrimination in employment. But employees alleging such discrimination have brought charges against employers on constitutional and other grounds.

Although the courts generally have held that an employee may not be discharged based solely on his status as a homosexual, they have upheld discharges for other reasons.

In a case in which the EEOC was the employer, the U.S. Court of Appeals for the Ninth Circuit held that the public flaunting and advocacy of homosexual conduct may be a valid reason for discharge. The employee contended that he was denied freedom of expression in violation of the First Amendment. But the EEOC successfully argued that the publicity linking the employee with the EEOC could cause "possible embarrassment to, and loss of public confidence in, the agency and the Federal Civil Service."

The court reasoned that the interest of the Government in promoting the efficiency of the public service outweighs the individual's First Amendment rights. It stressed that the discharge was upheld, based not on the employee's status as a homosexual, but rather for his public flaunting of a controversial life style, linked with his public identification as a federal employee. (Singer v. Civil Service Commission, 12 FEP Cases 208)

Off-Duty Conduct. A federal employee's discharge for an off-duty homosexual advance was held to be unlawful by the U.S. Court of Appeals for the District of Columbia.

The employee was observed making a pickup in the early morning hours. Police followed him back to his apartment and questioned him. He admitted that he had been involved in other homosexual encounters. But because there was nothing to suggest a reasonable connection between the evidence and the "efficiency of the service," the court decided that a discharge based on private

38

conduct during off-duty hours was unlawful. (Norton v. Macy, 9 FEP Cases 1382) A similar ruling led the Civil Service Commission to abandon its policy of automatic disqualification of known homosexuals. (Society for Individual Rights v. Hampton, 11 FEP Cases 1243)

Transfer From Teaching Position. A teacher who was transferred to an administrative position when it became known that he was a homosexual contended that the transfer violated his free speech rights under the First Amendment.

A lower court held that the transfer was justified because of public statements the teacher had made about homosexuality. The U.S. Court of Appeals for the Fourth Circuit disagreed with this reasoning, stating that it would impinge on free speech.

But the court upheld the transfer because the teacher had falsified information on his application form. The court decided that it was not necessary to consider the constitutionality of the application form because the teacher was barred from challenging what he had attempted to circumvent. The case involved the Board of Education of Montgomery County. (9 FEP Cases 1287)

Statutory Protection. Neither the Federal Government nor any state government has adopted a law protecting employees against discrimination because of homosexuality. But several local governments have laws or ordinances protecting individuals against employment discrimination based on sexual "orientation" or "deviation."

The most comprehensive local law was that adopted by the District of Columbia in 1973. This law forbids employment discrimination "for any reason other than that of individual merit." The forbidden bases of discrimination include, but are not limited to, the following: "Race, color, religion, national origin, sex, age, marital status, personal appearance, sexual orientation, family responsibilities, matriculation, political affiliation, physical handicap, source of income, and place of residence or business." (FEP 451:261)

SEXUAL HARASSMENT

The courts are split on whether sexual harassment on the job is sex discrimination.

Two appeals courts have found that a female employee has a Title VII claim if her employment status is prejudiced because she rejected the sexual advances of her supervisor. The U.S. Court of Appeals for the District of Columbia has held that a Title VII violation is established if gender is a factor contributing in a substantial way to discrimination. (Barnes v. Costle, 15 FEP Cases 345) And the Fourth Circuit has ruled that an employer violates Title VII when it fails to take prompt and appropriate remedial action upon learning that a supervisor has made sexual advances toward a subordinate employee and conditioned that employee's job status—evaluation, continued employment, promotion, or other aspects of career development—on a favorable response to those advances. (Garber v. Saxon Business Products, 15 FEP Cases 344)

A district court said there could be sex discrimination not only where a male supervisor approaches a female subordinate, but also where a female supervisor imposes sexual demands upon male subordinates, or where a homosexual supervisor makes demands on workers of the same sex. But the court added that there could be no finding of sex discrimination if the supervisor were bisexual and approached workers of both sexes equally. (Williams v. Saxbe, 12 FEP Cases 1093)

On the other hand, several district courts have decided that sexual harassment does not fall under Title VII. One court said sexual harassment is a matter of personal proclivity, peculiarity, or mannerism and not a company-directed policy to deprive women of employment opportunities. Nothing in Title VII, the court added, prohibits verbal and physical sexual advances by another employee where the conduct has no relationship to the nature of the employment. (Corne v. Bausch & Lomb, Inc., 10 FEP Cases 289)

40

Following a similar line of reasoning, another district court held that, unless there was a consistent policy of requiring female employees to submit to sexual advances by male supervisors, courts should not delve into isolated complaints of sexual misconduct as violations of Title VII.

If an isolated case of sexual harassment could succeed as a Title VII violation, the court said, there would be no end to allegations of sex-motivated considerations in cases of lost promotions, transfers, demotions, and dismissals. (Miller v. Bank of America, 13 FEP Cases 439)

RELIGIOUS DISCRIMINATION

In the 1972 amendments to Title VII, Congress added a definition of "religion" to aid the courts in applying the prohibition of employment discrimination based on religion.

The definition states: "The term 'religion' includes all aspects of religious observance and practice, as well as belief, unless an employer demonstrates that he is unable to reasonably accommodate to the employee's or prospective employee's religious observance or practice without undue hardship on the conduct of the employer's business."

In construing this amendment in a case involving General Dynamics, the Fifth Circuit rejected a contention that Congress intended to protect Sabbath observance only. The definition, it said, applies to all forms and aspects of religion except those that cannot be reconciled with a businesslike operation.

Cases involving the prohibition against religious discrimination have involved two principal issues:

► Whether an employer would have suffered an undue hardship if it had accommodated to an employee's need to be absent on a Sabbath beginning on Friday night and continuing until sundown on Saturday.

► Whether an employer and a union that enters into a union-shop or agency-shop agreement must attempt all reasonable accommodations to employees' beliefs that joining a union or paying fees to it is a violation of their religion.

SATURDAY SABBATH

Most of the cases involved the first issue. In the leading Dewey v. Reynolds Metals case, which went to the Supreme Court, the Sixth Circuit decided that the company did not violate Title VII by discharging an employee who refused because of his religion to work on Sunday or to arrange for a replacement as required by the collective bargaining contract.

42

The Title VII definition including the "reasonable accommodation" provision was not in effect at the time. Nor were the EEOC guidelines that included such a provision.

But even if they had been in effect, the court said, it would have ruled that the company made a reasonable accommodation to the employee's religious beliefs by offering to permit him to obtain a replacement. Moreover, his refusal placed an undue hardship on the company because of the necessity to require compulsory overtime to handle increased orders. The court added, however, that the "reasonable accommodation" provision in the EEOC guideline was inconsistent with Title VII as it read prior to the 1972 amendment. (2 FEP Cases 687, 869) The Sixth Circuit decision was affirmed by an equally divided Supreme Court. (3 FEP Cases 508) Because of the absence of a majority, the Supreme Court's holding was not a binding precedent.

Subsequent to the decision in the Dewey case, a number of circuits recognized the "reasonable accommodation" and "undue hardship" tests in resolving charges of religious discrimination. (10 FEP Cases 974, 11 FEP Cases 1106, 11 FEP Cases 1121)

But in the fall of 1976, the Supreme Court, again by an equally divided Court, upheld a decision reached by the U.S. Court of Appeals for the Sixth Circuit that an employer violated the provision of the 1972 definition of religion requiring the employer to make a reasonable accommodation to the religious practices of an employee when it discharged a supervisor who refused, for religious reasons, to work on Saturdays. The case involved the Parker Seal Co. Again, the Supreme Court's holding was not a binding precedent because of the absence of a majority. (13 FEP Cases 1178)

The Supreme Court finally resolved the issues in June 1977. It made these rulings:

▶ An employer is not required to take steps inconsistent with a contractual seniority system to accommodate the religious practices of an employee who refuses to work on Saturdays.

▶ To require an employer to bear more than a *de minimis* cost to give the employee Saturdays off, is an undue hardship within the meaning of Title VII.

The collective bargaining contract specified that the most senior employees should have first choice for job and shift preference and that the most junior employees were required to work when the union steward was unable to find enough people to work at a particular time or in a particular job to fill the employer's needs.

Noting that the emphasis of Title VII is on eliminating discrimination in employment, the Court stated that it would be "anomalous" to conclude that Congress meant that an employer must deny the shift and job preference of some employees, as well as deprive them of their contractual rights, to accommodate the religious needs of others. (Trans World Air Lines, Inc. v. Hardison, 14 FEP Cases 1697)

UNION SECURITY

Prior to the adoption of Title VII, employees who objected to union security contracts on religious grounds attacked the contracts under the First Amendment to the Constitution, the Railway Labor Act, or the Taft-Hartley Act. They failed in every case. (9 FEP Cases 243, 9 FEP Cases 245, 1 FEP Cases 256, 9 FEP Cases 266, 9 FEP Cases 275) Since Title VII was adopted, attacks also have been made under its provisions.

Like the cases involving religious discrimination based on refusal to grant variances in work schedules, those involving union security under Title VII also have been resolved under the "reasonable accommodation" and "undue hardship" tests.

In a major decision by the Fifth Circuit, the three-judge panel wrote three opinions. All three judges agreed that the duty of making a "reasonable accommodation" to the employee's religious beliefs applied to both the employer and the union. Two of the judges also held that the defense of "undue hardship" applied to the union as well as the employer.

But they differed on what would be a "reasonable accommodation." Two of the judges held that among the alternatives that should be considered is the possibility of permitting the employees to continue their regular work assignments without making any payments to the union.

The other judge reasoned that Title VII does not exempt persons with religious convictions from paying dues under an agency-shop contract. He suggested that the court explore whether an accommodation, such as transfer to an open shop, could be made without "undue hardship." The case involved General Dynamics. (12 FEP Cases 1549)

Other courts have made conflicting interpretations of "reasonable accommodation" and "undue hardship." For example:

► The Ninth Circuit in a case involving North American Rockwell held that the employer and the union must attempt an accommodation to an employee's religious beliefs, but it expressed doubt that any accommodation could be reached, appearing to say that any accommodation would have to include a payment by the employee in some form. (8 FEP Cases 546)

► A district court rejected the argument that the religious objections of a Seventh-Day Adventist to making payments to a union could be accommodated by requiring him to make payments to a charity. The employer would suffer undue hardship, the court said, because there would be dissension and friction involving other employees who would object to such an arrangement. And there would be undue hardship for the union because a decision in favor of the employee would encourage other Seventh-Day Adventists to seek employment with the employer, thus imposing a substantial financial hardship on the union. The case involved the Southern Pacific Transportation Co. (11 FEP Cases 1441)

► A Maine court found that a union, a local of the Papermakers, would suffer undue hardship if it were required to exempt a Seventh-Day Adventist from paying dues. But the court enjoined the employee's discharge until a determination could be made whether it would constitute undue hardship for her to be transferred outside the bargaining unit. (12 FEP Cases 192)

WEARING RELIGIOUS CLOTHING

Some questions have been raised about the legality of an employer's banning the wearing of certain religious clothing on the job. This has applied particularly to the Black Muslims.

In a case decided in 1974, a federal district court, on the basis of the pleadings, refused to dismiss a charge that Rollins, Inc., violated Title VII by not allowing a Black Muslim to wear certain clothing. (8 FEP Cases 492)

MINISTERIAL MEETINGS

Citing the Section 701(j) amendment to Title VII, a federal district court held that Title VII was applicable to an employer's discharge of an employee who missed work to attend his church's ministerial meetings.

The court referred to the broad definition of "religion" in Section 701(j) as embracing all aspects of religious observance and practice. The case involved Goodyear Tire and Rubber Co. (10 FEP Cases 513)

ATHEIST AND DEVOTIONAL SERVICE

In an unusual case involving Southwestern Savings and Loan Association and an atheist, the Fifth Circuit held that the atheist was constructively discharged in violation of Title VII when she resigned after being told by her supervisor that she must attend monthly staff meetings that began with a devotional service. The court said that the employee reasonably could have inferred from her supervisor's remarks that she would be discharged if her absence at the devotional service was noticed. (10 FEP Cases 522)

At the time the original Title VII was being considered, an exemption to permit employers to discriminate against atheists was proposed. But it was deleted as being of "doubtful constitutionality."

NATIONAL ORIGIN, ALIENAGE DISCRIMINATION

The term "national origin" is not defined in Title VII or other federal statutes or orders relating to employment discrimination. But it has come to mean the country of a person's ancestry, rather than race or color. It also is related in the cases to matters of alienage.

The majority of the cases have involved Spanish-surnamed Americans—a group including Mexican-Americans, Puerto Ricans, and others of Spanish heritage. The aliens involved in the cases have been primarily Mexican or Chinese.

EEOC GUIDELINES

The EEOC has issued guidelines on discrimination based on national origin. (FEP 401:201) The guidelines make the following points:

► Although Title VII contains a bona fide occupational qualification (BFOQ) exception for national origin cases, this exception will be strictly construed.

► The EEOC will examine "with particular concern" cases involving national origin discrimination of a covert nature. This includes, for example, discrimination against an individual because of a characteristic peculiar to his heritage.

► Discrimination against a lawfully domiciled alien amounts to discrimination for citizenship and so for national origin. (FEP 401:34) But in Espinoza v. Farah Manufacturing Co., the Supreme Court ruled that aliens are not protected by Title VII and, on this reasoning, upheld a company's long-standing policy of not hiring aliens. (6 FEP Cases 933) After the Espinoza decision, a registered alien filed an action against the Manchester Terminal Corp. and a union under both Title VII and the 1866 Act (42 U.S.C. Sec.

47

1981). Although the Fifth Circuit held that the alleged discrimination did not violate Title VII, it violated Section 1981 as discriminating against Spanish-surnamed Americans or aliens of Mexican origin. (8 FEP Cases 433)

In another case, Caucasian American citizens sued a Japanese-owned American corporation, alleging unlawful discrimination under both Title VII and Section 1981. The court upheld the right of the plaintiffs to sue under both laws. (Spiess v. C. Itoh & Co., 12 FEP Cases 230)

Prior to the Manchester Terminal case, the Supreme Court held in the Sugarman case that the Equal Protection Clause of the Constitution barred a state from excluding a resident alien from the state's competitive civil service. (5 FEP Cases 1152) The EEOC's guidelines state that local and state laws prohibiting the employment of noncitizens are in conflict with and so superseded by Title VII. (FEP 401:34)

In Hampton v. Wong decided by the Supreme Court in 1976, the principle was extended to the Federal Government. The Court held a Civil Service Commission regulation that indiscriminatorily excluded all aliens from all civil service positions is unconstitutional as depriving resident-aliens of liberty without due process of law—a violation of the Fifth Amendment. (12 FEP Cases 1377)

HEIGHT, WEIGHT RESTRICTIONS

Physical restrictions that have the effect of denying employment to a certain class of persons who tend to be below the general norm for height and weight may be held discriminatory if they cannot be proved to be related directly to the work involved.

The requirement of an oil tool manufacturer that all production employees be at least 5'5" tall, for example, was considered discriminatory by the EEOC. The Commission said that the height excluded a significantly larger proportion of women and Spanish-surnamed American men than Caucasian men. EEOC added that the employer failed to show that the height requirement was necessary to the safe and efficient operation of the company so as to justify its discriminatory effects. (EEOC Decision, May 9, 1971, Decision No. 71-1529, 3 FEP Cases 952)

LANGUAGE DIFFICULTIES

Unless an employer can prove that flawless, unaccented English is a requirement of the job, the EEOC may find that the employer engaged in national origin discrimination. It was considered a violation by the EEOC where a Spanish-surnamed American employee was discharged on the employer's claim that the employee had a "communications barrier" inconsistent with the operation of the business. The employer's "clear communications" criterion, the EEOC said, disqualified a significantly larger proportion of Spanish-surnamed Americans than non-Spanish-surnamed Americans. It added that the employee's previous work experience required him to communicate in English and that his co-workers had no difficulty understanding him, despite his noticeable Spanish accept. (EEOC Sixth Annual Report, Decision No. 71-1912)

See above under "Discrimination by Employers on the Basis of Race: Employment Conditions" for a discussion of a case involving an employer's rule banning the use of the Spanish language in the plant during both working and nonworking time.

NATIONAL ORIGIN HARASSMENT

It is EEOC's position that an employer is required to maintain a working atmosphere free of ethnic and racial harassment. Moreover, this requirement sometimes calls for positive action by the employer directed toward those employees who are harassing others.

In a case in which a foreign-born employee was the butt of "Polish jokes" and generally derogatory remarks about his ancestry from co-workers, EEOC found that the employer engaged in discrimination on the basis of national origin. Despite the statements of co-workers that the charging party was hypersensitive, EEOC ruled that "tolerance by first-line supervisors of national origin ridicule may not be condoned as a common or allowable condition of employment." (EEOC Decision, No. CLG8-12-431EU)

RETALIATION

Like some of the other major federal labor laws, including the Taft-Hartley and Fair Labor Standards Acts, Title VII contains a prohibition against retaliation.

Section 704(g) makes it an unlawful employment practice to discriminate against any employee, union member, or applicant for employment or union membership because he has opposed an unlawful employment practice or has filed a charge, testified, assisted, or participated in any manner in an investigation, proceeding, or hearing under Title VII.

The prohibition applies to employers, employment agencies, labor unions, and joint labor-management committees controlling apprenticeship or other training or retraining programs.

INJUNCTIVE RELIEF

The provisions forbidding retaliatory action are not self-enforcing. For this reason, Congress in the 1972 amendments gave the EOCC and the Attorney General authority to seek temporary injunctive relief to preserve the status quo where there is an allegation of unlawful retaliatory action. But the Fifth Circuit held that the 1972 amendment didn't take away the preexisting right of an employee to go into court and seek such relief on his own based on an allegation of retaliatory action for filing a charge with the EEOC. (Drew v. Liberty Mutual Insurance Co., 5 FEP Cases 1077)

SCOPE OF PROTECTION

According to the Fifth Circuit a person filing charges of discrimination against his employer is protected against retaliation even if those charges are false or malicious. (Pettway v. American Cast Iron Pipe Co., 1 FEP Cases 752)

But the First Circuit decided that the protection against retaliation under Section 704(a) does not give an employee unlimited license to complain of alleged discrimination. Upholding a lower court finding that the employee's discharge was not a violation, the court explained that a balance must be reached between the purpose of protecting persons engaging reasonably in activities opposing discrimination and Congress' equally manifest desire not to tie the hands of employers in objective selection and control of personnel. (Hochstadt v. Worcester Foundation, 13 FEP Cases 804)

EXAMPLES OF RETALIATION

In the eyes of the EEOC, retaliation violations are particularly serious. First, they work a great hardship upon the individual involved. Second, they have a long-term chilling effect upon the willingness of others to oppose Title VII discrimination. For this reason the EEOC and the courts have construed the protection broadly.

Here are some examples of holdings on retaliation:

► An employer engaged in unlawful retaliation by refusing to process an employment application until the applicant, who had filed a charge with the EEOC against another company, settled his dispute with that company. (Barela v. United Nuclear Corp., 4 FEP Cases 831)

► An employer violated Title VII by harassing an employee who had filed a charge with the EEOC by directing supervisors to build a case against her and to apply a pattern of oppressive supervision over her. (Francis v. AT&T, 4 FEP Cases 777)

► A violation was found when a medical clinic, after being ordered by Medicaid officials to integrate its segregated patient reception and waiting rooms, discharged the sole black receptionist when the integration permitted reduction in the number of required receptionists by one. (EEOC Decision, March 6, 1973, No. 72-1267, 4 FEP Cases 710)

► An employer was held to have engaged in unlawful discrimination where an employee who filed a charge against the employer thereafter was assigned to "erratic and undesirable working hours." (EEOC Decision, September 15, 1976, No. 72-0455, 4 FEP Cases 306)

► In two separate cases, violations were found where employees were discharged for objection to (1) a supervisor harassing employees by preaching on the job, and (2) a company's mandatory religious meetings. (EEOC Decision, Feb. 18, 1972, No. 72114, 4 FEP Cases 842; EEOC Decision, December 17, 1971, No. 72-0528, 4 FEP Cases 434)

AGE DISCRIMINATION

Enacted in 1967, the Age Discrimination in Employment Act (ADEA) seeks to promote the employment of older persons based upon their ability instead of their age. It originally prohibited discrimination in employment against persons between the ages of 40 and 65. In 1978, the law was amended to prohibit discrimination against those between the ages of 40 and 70. For employees then under 65, the amendment became effective April 6, 1978; for those then between 65 and 69, the amendment became effective January 1, 1979. For employees covered by a collective bargaining agreement in effect on September 1, 1977, however, the change is postponed until the termination of the contract or January 1, 1980, whichever occurs first.

Administration and enforcement of the Act originally were entrusted to the Department of Labor. But in 1978 these functions were transferred to the EEOC, effective July 1, 1979.

COVERAGE OF ADEA

Like Title VII of the Civil Right Act, ADEA applies to employers, employment agencies, labor organizations, and federal, state, and local government. The scope of coverage is determined by these definitions:

► *Employer* is defined as a person engaged in an industry affecting commerce who has 20 or more employees for each working day in each of 20 or more calendar weeks in the current or preceding calendar year.

► *Person* is defined to include "one or more individuals, partnerships, associations, labor organizations, corporations, business trusts, legal representatives, or any organized group of persons."

► *Industry affecting commerce* is defined as "any activity, business or industry in commerce or in which a labor dispute would hinder or obstruct commerce or the free flow of commerce and includes any activity directly or indirectly 'affecting commerce' within the meaning of the Landrum-Griffin Act of 1959."

▶ *Employment agency* is defined as any person regularly undertaking with or without compensation to procure employees for an employer. It also includes an agent of such a person, but it does not include an agent of the United States.

▶ *Labor organization* is defined the same way it is defined in Title VII of the Equal Employment Opportunity Act. The tests are maintaining or operating a hiring hall, being certified or recognized as a bargaining representative, chartering a local labor organization, or being chartered by a labor organization.

▶ *Employee* is defined broadly to include any individual employed by an employer. But there are exemptions for state and municipal officials, appointees of such officials on a policy-making level, and immediate advisers with respect to the official's exercise of his constitutional or legal powers. Although the Act defines "employee" as a person employed by an employer, the interpretive bulletin issued by the Labor Department states that it clearly was intended by Congress that the term should include an applicant for employment.

Although the Supreme Court struck down as unconstitutional the 1974 amendments to the Fair Labor Standards Act that extended minimum wage and overtime pay coverage to state and local government employees, the application of ADEA to such employees has been upheld. (Usery v. Board of Education of Salt Lake City, 13 FEP Cases 717)

FORBIDDEN DISCRIMINATION

The prohibitions of ADEA parallel those under Title VII.

Employers of 20 or more persons are forbidden to do any of the following:

▶ Fail or refuse to hire, discharge, or otherwise discriminate against any individual because of his age with respect to compensation, terms, conditions, or privileges of employment.

▶ Limit, segregate, or classify an employee in any way that would deprive him of job opportunities or adversely affect his employment status because of age.'

▶ Reduce the wage rate of an employee to comply with the Act.

► Indicate any "preference, limitation, specification, or discrimination" based on age in any notices or advertisements for employment.

The prohibitions also apply to employment agencies serving covered employees and labor unions with 25 or more members.

Employment agencies are forbidden to fail or refuse to refer individuals for employment because of age. Unions are forbidden to expel or exclude persons from membership on the basis of age.

EXCEPTIONS

As under Title VII, ADEA provides for a number of exceptions. The prohibitions do not apply if based on one or more of the following:

► A "bona fide occupational qualification" (BFOQ) that is reasonably necessary to the normal operation of the business.

► A differentiation based on reasonable factors other than age.

► A bona fide seniority system or employee benefit plan, provided that no such benefit plan shall excuse the failure to hire any individual because of age.

► Discharge or other disciplinary action against an individual for good cause.

APPLICATION OF RULES

The prohibitions under the Act apply only when one of the employees involved in the alleged discrimination is in the 40-70 age bracket.

But there still may be unlawful discrimination if both employees are within the age bracket. If, for example, an employee aged 50 claims he is being discriminated against in favor of an employee aged 45, there could be a violation. (FEP 401:403)

An employer legally may indicate a preference for a worker at least 40 but less than 65 (70 under the 1978 amendment), according to the Wage and Hour Division. But a preference for a specific age range—such as 40 to 50—would not be legal. (FEP 401:403)

HELP-WANTED ADS

In view of the Labor Department, no indication of a preference based on age may be included in a help-wanted ad. Included in the ban are such terms as "age 25 to 35," "under 40," or descriptive words such as "young," "boy," or "girl." But this does not bar specifying a minimum age that is less than 40.

The interpretations of the Labor Department have been litigated with mixed results. For example:

▶ An employment agency, Career Counsellors Int'l, Inc., was found to have violated ADEA by placing "help-wanted" advertisements in newspapers indicating preference for a "girl." Stating that the Labor Department's interpretation was entitled to "great deference," the court said that the ads indicated a prejudice against individuals over 40. (5 FEP Cases 129)

▶ But in another case, the Paragon Employment Agency published an advertisement for "college students," "girls," "boys," and "June graduates," and a court found no illegal age discrimination. The court said that the Act does not forbid employers from encouraging young persons from turning from idleness to useful endeavor. (5 FEP Cases 915, 7 FEP Cases 1258)

▶ Help-wanted advertisements directed to "recent graduates" did not automatically violate ADEA, according to a ruling by the Fourth Circuit Court of Appeals. If the ads are part of a general invitation to a specific class of prospective customers coming into the job market at a particular time of the year, the court said, there is no violation. But if the phrase is used in reference to a specific job opportunity, there would be a violation of the Act as implying older persons need not apply. The effect is determined by the context, not the words. (Hodgson v. Approved Personnel Service, 11 FEP Cases 688)

EMPLOYMENT TESTS

Tests may be used in hiring and promotion. But they must be validated as (1) specifically related to the requirements of the job, (2) fair and reasonable, (3) administered in good faith and without discrimination on the basis of age, and (4) properly evaluated.

Because of the increasing use of tests, younger workers tend to be more "test-sophisticated" than older workers. For this reason, the Labor Department will scrutinize the selection procedure closely where tests are the only determining factor. (See FEP 421:355)

BFOQ EXCEPTION

An exception to the Act provides that there will be no violation where age is a bona fide occupational qualification for a job. Some examples of possible BFOQ exceptions are:

► Federal statutory and regulatory requirements that impose a compulsory age limitation, such as the Federal Aviation Agency regulation setting a ceiling of age 60 for pilots.

► Actors required for youthful or elderly roles.

► Persons used to advertise or promote the sale of products designed for youthful or elderly consumers.

► A bus line's maximum-age hiring policy for intercity drivers, since a public carrier might continually strive to employ the most qualified persons available and since the essence of the business is the safe transportation of passengers. (See Usery v. Tamiani Trail Tours, 12 FEP Cases 1233.)

FACTORS OTHER THAN AGE

There also is an exception for "reasonable factors other than age."

Physical fitness requirements based on preemployment or periodic physical examinations related to standards reasonably necessary for the specific job and uniformly required will be upheld, for example.

The same is true of evaluation factors, such as quality or quantity of production, or educational levels, where the factors have a valid relationship to the job and are uniformly applied, as noted in cases involving Monsanto and Union Carbide. (3 FEP Cases 22, 7 FEP Cases 571)

Seniority Systems. Such systems which are bona fide and not "a subterfuge to evade the purposes of the Act" also may be observed without violating the age discrimination prohibition.

But the seniority system must make length of service the primary criterion for allocating work opportunities and prerogatives. Moreover, it must be communicated to all employees and be uniformly applied. (FEP 401:5081)

Employee Pension, Benefit Plans. If an employer has a "bona fide" pension or benefit plan, he will not be required to provide older workers with the same pension or insurance benefits as provided to younger workers.

Moreover, early retirement—or even involuntary early retirement—does not violate the Act, provided it is within the terms of a pension plan that meets the requirements of the Act. The Supreme Court upheld the involuntary retirement of a 60-year-old employee in a case involving United Air Lines, finding that the retirement was pursuant to a bona fide pension plan. (16 FEP Cases 146)

ENFORCEMENT

As under Title VII, ADEA stresses voluntary compliance with the Act's provisions. The Secretary of Labor is directed to seek compliance through the informal methods of conciliation, conference, and persuasion.

But if efforts to obtain voluntary compliance fail, an aggrieved individual may bring an action in any court of competent jurisdiction for such legal or equitable relief as will effectuate the purposes of the Act. Class actions are not authorized.

The Secretary of Labor also may sue for legal or equitable relief. The court may grant an injunction to restrain violations and may award back pay in the form of minimum wages or overtime pay. Liquidated damages, however, may be awarded only where "willful" violations are found. The courts are divided on whether either compensatory or punitive damages may be awarded.

Suits by aggrieved individuals are subject to these provisions:

▶ The individual must give the Secretary not less than 60 days' notice of an intent to file an action.

▶ The notice of intent to sue must be filed within 180 days after the alleged unlawful practice occurred.

▶ Where the alleged violation takes place in a state that has an age discrimination law, the notice of intent to bring an action must be filed within 300 days after the alleged unlawful practice occurred or within 30 days after the receipt of the notice of termination of proceedings under the state law, whichever is earlier.

▶ When the Secretary of Labor receives a notice of intent to sue, he is required to notify all prospective defendants and to seek to eliminate any alleged unlawful practice by the informal methods of conciliation, conference, and persuasion.

► The filing of a suit by the Secretary terminates the individual's right to sue.

The two-year statute of limitations under the Portal-to-Portal Act applies to claims under ADEA, although the time limit is three years when the alleged violation is willful. The good-faith defense provisions under the Portal Act also apply under ADEA.

Although ADEA contains no provision expressly granting a jury trial, it is available in private action for lost wages, the Supreme Court has ruled. (16 FEP Cases 885)

Employers, unions, and employment agencies are required to maintain certain records and to make them available for inspection by representatives of the Labor Department.

HANDICAPPED-WORKER DISCRIMINATION

In 1973, Congress enacted the Vocational Rehabilitation Act. Section 503 requires employers with federal contracts over $2,500 to take affirmative action for the employment of handicapped persons.

Although discrimination against the handicapped is a relatively new area in equal employment opportunity, there are similarities to the rules against discrimination on the basis of race, sex, and national origin.

But there also are significant differences. There are, for example, no numerical hiring goals that must be achieved. Although there is no requirement that an unqualified person be hired, affirmative action does require that an employer take steps to accommodate a handicapped worker unless such accommodation imposes an "undue hardship" on the employer.

DEFINITION

The Act defines a handicapped individual as a person "who has a physical or mental impairment which substantially limits one or more of such person's major life activities." According to the Labor Department's definition, such a limitation may be evidenced if the individual is likely to experience difficulty in obtaining, retaining, or advancing in employment because of a handicap.

The Act also considers as handicapped those individuals who have a record of such an impairment or are "regarded as having" an impairment. An individual who may be recovered completely from a previous mental or physical impairment (such as mentally restored or recovered from a heart attack or cancer) may have difficulty in obtaining or holding a job because of his handicap history. He receives protection under the Act as also do those erroneously classified as handicapped.

EXEMPTIONS

All contracts under $2,500 automatically are exempt from the affirmative action requirement. Moreover, while American citizens working overseas in business with covered federal contracts are protected by the Act, foreigners working in the same business are not protected. Whether employees of conglomerates are covered depends on the exact nature of the corporate arrangement and the nature of the government contract.

Waiver of Affirmative Action. A waiver of the affirmative action obligation may be granted by the head of a contracting agency to an otherwise covered employer where the waiver is deemed to be in the "national interest" or in the "interest of national security." Where the contention is "national interest," the Secretary of Labor must concur in the waiver, but he need not where the claim is "national security."

The affirmative action requirements also may be waived at any of the contractor's facilities found to be "in all respects separate and distinct" from the facilities related to the performances of the government contract. The waiver will be considered, however, only if requested by the contractor or subcontractor.

AFFIRMATIVE ACTION

A company has 120 days after the award of a covered contract to prepare an affirmative action program covering the handicapped. There is no obligation to submit the program to the Government. But it must be available for inspection by any employee or applicant, and the employer must post in a conspicuous place in the plant a notice of its affirmative action obligations.

The Labor Department's regulations on the handicapped emphasize recruitment and communication of the employer's policy on hiring the handicapped. But goals or quotas are not required.

Here are some of the major provisions regarding affirmative action programs for the handicapped, as specified by the Labor Department's regulations (FEP 401:641):

► In recruiting, the scope of the employer's efforts "shall depend upon all the circumstances, including the contractor's size and resources and the extent to which existing employment practices are adequate." State rehabilitation agencies, sheltered workshops, schools for the handicapped, and social service agencies are suggested as sources.

▶ Contractors are to provide in their affirmative action programs a schedule for review of all physical or mental job qualification requirements to ensure that, to the extent they screen out qualified handicapped persons, they are job-related and consistent with business necessity and the safe performance of the job.

▶ Employers still may conduct physical examinations of applicants, as long as they are not used to exclude qualified handicapped persons. Any inquiries as to an applicant's or employee's physical or mental condition are to be kept confidential except that: (1) Supervisors may be informed regarding work restrictions and accommodations that may be necessary; (2) first aid and medical personnel may be informed if the condition might require emergency treatment; and (3) government officials investigating compliance shall be informed.

▶ Each covered employer must maintain records on complaints, compliance reviews, and other required reports for one year. Affirmative action programs must be brought up to date annually.

ENFORCEMENT

Failure by a contractor or subcontractor to comply with the regulations may result in judicial enforcement, debarment from future government contracts, contract termination, or withholding of contract payments "as necessary to correct any violations."

Any applicant or employee may file a complaint alleging a violation with the Department of Labor. The charge must be filed within 180 days of the date of the alleged violation. The Department first refers the complaint to the employer for internal review. If the employer and the complainant are unable to resolve the problem within 60 days, the Department procedures go into effect.

Under these procedures, the Labor Department investigates the complaints and attempts to obtain compliance by the employer "through conciliation and persuasion within a reasonable time." If the informal means are unsuccessful in resolving the violation, the contractor is given the opportunity for a formal hearing. The hearing officer will make recommendations, and final action will be taken by the Office of Federal Contract Compliance Programs.

COURT DECISIONS

In deciding cases involving discrimination against handicapped workers, the courts have tended to rely upon constitutional guarantees and state laws, rather than the Rehabilitation Act, which, it has been held, does not provide for a private cause of action. (16 FEP Cases 20, 14 FEP Cases 1752)

The courts have considered the following factors:

► Whether an employee presently is able to do the job.

► Whether an employee's disease is degenerative and will prevent him from performing in the future.

► Whether an employer is required to hire or maintain handicapped workers who are unable to meet company performance standards.

► To what extent the company must make reasonable accommodations for handicapped workers.

Some examples of court decisions are as follows:

► In a case involving Milwaukee Road, an employee newly hired was found to have been terminated unlawfully under the Wisconsin State Fair Employment Act because he had a history of asthma. The court said the termination violated the Act because the employee was in the protected group of handicapped in that, although his disease made achievement difficult, he still was capable of performing the work efficiently. (8 FEP Cases 938)

► A Pennsylvania school district violated the Due Process Clause of the Constitution by refusing to consider a blind applicant for a position as a secondary school English teacher. The summary rejection of the application, the court said, created a presumption that blind persons cannot be competent teachers for students with sight. (14 FEP Cases 1359)

► In a case involving the Boeing Company, an electronics technican suffered from cerebral palsy. It limited his physical coordination, but not his mental abilities.

During a reduction in force, the employee was transferred to a different section that required skills and coordination he did not possess. Because of unsatisfactory work, he was offered a choice of a job at four pay grades lower or termination. He took the lower grade job.

A court found that the employee had been discriminated against based on his disability, in violation of the Washington State Law Against Discrimination in Employment. Placing the employee in a job he could perform, the court said, would not place an undue burden on the company. Awarding the employee back pay and legal fees, the court explained that the transfer to the other department was not the only option open to the company. (12 FEP Cases 975)

ALCOHOL, DRUGS

The Labor Department has taken the position that alcoholics and drug abusers are within the protection of the Vocational Rehabilitation Act.

It was the intention of Congress to cover these two groups, the Department said. The Office of Federal Contract Compliance, which administers the Act, had processed 11 complaints involving alcoholism and six involving drug abuse by 1977. It has emphasized, however, that an employer must hire and promote only "qualified handicapped workers."

EQUAL PAY ACT

The Equal Pay Act was passed in 1963 as an amendment to Section 6 of the Fair Labor Standards Act. Its objective was to eliminate wage differentials based on sex. Since Title VII forbids all employment discrimination based on sex, there is some overlapping under the two laws.

But the prohibitions under Title VII are broader, extending to employment conditions that go beyond wages. Moreover, as part of the Fair Labor Standards Act, the Equal Pay Act is subject to the exemptions in the basic statute, including those for executive, administrative, and professional employees and outside salesmen. Such employees are subject to Title VII.

Administration of the Act originally was entrusted to the Labor Department's Wage-Hour Division. But in 1978 this function was transferred to the EEOC, effective July 1, 1979.

EQUAL-PAY STANDARD

Under the equal-pay standard, it is unlawful for an employer to pay wages "at a rate less than the rate at which he pays employees of the opposite sex in such establishments for equal work on jobs the performance of which require equal skill, effort, and responsibility, and which are performed under similar working conditions."

So, *skill, effort, responsibility, and working conditions* are tests of equality of work. But to be considered "substantially equal," jobs are not required to be identical.

In a leading case, the Third Circuit found a company in violation of the Equal Pay Act for basing wage differentials on "an artificially created job classification," which the court found clearly appeared to have been intended to keep women in a subordinate role. (Shultz v. Wheaton Glass Co., 19 WH Cases 336)

EXCEPTIONS

There is a general exception in the Act for wage differentials based on any factor other than sex. There are specific exemptions for:

► Wage differentials paid pursuant to a seniority system.

► Wage differentials paid pursuant to a merit system.

► Wage differentials paid pursuant to a system that measures earnings by quantity or quality of production.

The three specific exceptions are not limited to formal systems or plans that are reduced to writing. Informal or unwritten plans may qualify if it can be demonstrated that the standards have been applied pursuant to an established plan whose terms have been communicated to the employees.

But when investigating possible violations, the Government will check to assure that, although the formal specifications of a merit system may be nondiscriminatory in appearance, they actually are also applied in a nondiscriminatory manner.

So under this reasoning, the factor of sex may not provide any part of the basis for the wage differential. Any seniority or merit system that establishes separate standards for men and without regard to job content will be carefully examined.

INTERPRETATIVE BULLETIN

The Wage-Hour Administrator has issued guidelines in the form of an interpretative bulletin. The bulletin may be found at FEP 401:601. The Wage-Hour Division issues opinion letters that supplement the bulletin. Some of the major points made in the bulletin and opinion letters follow:

► When applied without distinction to employees of both sexes, no equal-pay problems are presented by shift differentials, incentive payments, production bonuses, performance and longevity raises, and the like.

► "Part-time workers do not have to be paid the same wage as full-time workers of the opposite sex." But there must be a distinction between part-time and full-time work—a cutoff of 20 hours a week for part-time workers, for example. (Wage-Hour Opinion Letter, April 9, 1965)

► Differentials such as higher pay ratios for "heads of families," provided they are made equally to men and women in the same category. But they will not be permitted if they are being used merely as a guise for giving men a higher rate. (Wage-Hour Opinion Letter, July 21, 1964)

► A higher pay scale for men than for women who perform equal work usually will not be justified, even if the employer finds that the average cost of employing a woman is higher than that of employing a man. Before such an exception could be justified, a complete investigation and analysis would have to be completed. This would have to show more than the additional pension and benefit costs for women employees. (Wage-Hour Opinion Letter, June 18, 1964)

► A wage differential may not be justified on the ground that the average production of one sex as a group is lower than the average production of the other sex. To group solely on the basis of sex for comparison purposes necessarily rests on the assumption that the sex factors alone may justify a wage differential—an assumption clearly contrary to the terms and purposes of the statute. Such a practice would penalize all employees of one sex without regard to the production of any one individual of either sex. (Wage-Hour Opinion Letter, June 6, 1970)

► Wage classification systems that may have the effect of treating men and women differently in pay, as well as other aspects of employment, by designation of certain jobs as "male jobs" and others as "female jobs" may violate both the Equal Pay Act and Title VII of the Civil Rights Act. (Wage-Hour Opinion Letter, June 6, 1970)

WHAT IS 'ESTABLISHMENT'?

The Equal Pay Act requires that comparisons be made only between wages paid employees of the opposite sex in the same establishment. There is no need to compare rates paid in different establishments.

So the definition of an "establishment" is critical to the application of the equal-pay standard. Although "establishment" is not expressly defined in the Equal Pay Act, it has the same meaning as it has under other sections of the Fair Labor Standards Act.

As defined in the interpretative bulletin, "establishment" refers to a "distinct physical place of business," rather than to "an entire enterprise or business," which may include several places of business.

On this basis, the Wage-Hour Division found that two divisions that were semi-autonomous were separate establishments where:

► Each was physically separated from the other's activities;

► They were functionally operated as separate units with separate records and separate bookkeeping; *and*

► There was no interchange of employees between the units —except on a minimal or emergency basis. (Wage-Hour Opinion Letter, June 7, 1966)

WHAT ARE WAGES?

In comparing wages, the term is given the same meaning as it is under other provisions of the Fair Labor Standards Act.

Wages include "all payments made to or on behalf of the employee as remuneration for employment." Included are all rates whether calculated on a time, piece, job, incentive, or other basis. It also includes the rate for overtime pay. Although the use of different methods to compute overtime pay for men and women would not of itself be a violation of the equal-pay standards, the results must provide equal pay for equal work. (Wage-Hour Opinion Letter, December 14, 1964)

Holiday pay also is considered "remuneration for employment" and is covered under the equal-pay provisions. So men and women must receive equal pay for holidays worked and not worked. (Wage-Hour Opinion Letter, February 4, 1965)

WHAT IS EQUAL WORK?

The equality of work performed by men and women is determined on the basis of the "skill, effort, and responsibility" required and on the similarity of working conditions. To be considered "substantially equal," jobs need not be identical. Nor must they be performed with the same frequency. (See Brennan v. Owensboro County Hospital, 11 FEP Cases 600.)

In applying these tests, Wage-Hour investigators generally will scrutinize the job as a whole and look at the characteristics of the jobs being compared over the full work cycle.

Application of the equal-pay standard is not dependent on "classifications, point values, or job titles, but on actual job require-

ments and performance. Job content is the controlling factor."
(Wage-Hour Opinion Letter, Aug. 12, 1970)

In the leading Wheaton Glass case, the Third Circuit held
unlawful a 21½ cents an hour differential in favor of men "selec-
tor-packers." The company contended that the differential was
justified by the fact that the men occasionally were required to
perform heavier work (9 FEP Cases 502); see also above under
"Equal-Pay Standard."

Similarly, the Fifth Circuit held that a bank violated the "substantially equal" provision of the Act when it paid men tellers more
than women tellers. The only extra duties of the men, the court
said, were to set break periods for outside tellers and to "look after
them" when they had problems. This occurred at most only once
a day and possibly at a rate of once a week. This was not enough
of a difference, the court said, to justify a differential in favor of the
men tellers. (Hodgson v. American Bank of Commerce, 9 FEP
Cases 677)

WHAT IS EQUAL SKILL?

The standard of equal skill is based upon the experiences,
training, education, and ability required in performing the job.

Two jobs will qualify as "equal" if they require essentially the
same skill even though the employee in one of the jobs may not
exercise the required skill as often as the employee in the other job.
Moreover, the efficiency of an employee's performance in the job is
not, in itself, an appropriate factor to consider in evaluating a skill.

There have been a number of cases involving the skill required
of women nursing aids and men orderlies. The issue was whether
more skill was required in the job of orderly, but a number of
courts held that the additional duties, responsibilities, or weight
lifting of the orderlies was not substantial (see cases listed at FEP
421:305).

But in two involving nursing home and hospital employees, the
Fifth Circuit stated that the issue of equality is a question of fact
to be decided on a case-by-case basis.

It affirmed a finding in the one case that the jobs were not
equal. (Hodgson v. Golden Isles Nursing Home, Inc., 9 FEP Cases
791) In the other, the court affirmed a finding that the jobs were
equal. (Hodgson v. Brookhaven General Hospital, 9 FEP Cases
579)

WHAT IS EQUAL EFFORT?

The rules on what is equal effort are related to those on equal work and equal skill. Although effort measures the physical and mental exertion required, jobs may require equal effort, even though the effort is exerted in different ways.

But even though jobs may involve most of the same routine tasks, they do not fall into the "equal effort" category "if the more highly paid jobs involve additional tasks that":

► Require extra effort;

► Consume a significant amount of time of all higher paid personnel; and

► Are of an economic value commensurate with the pay differential.

These standards were laid down by the Fifth Circuit in a case involving hospital employees. (Hodgson v. Brookhaven General Hospital, 9 FEP Cases 579) Higher pay for extra duties would not be justified, according to a ruling by the Sixth Circuit, where the extra task consumes only a minimal amount of time and is of peripheral importance. (Brennan v. Owensboro Davis County Hospital, 11 FEP Cases 600)

WHAT IS EQUAL RESPONSIBILITY?

The degree of accountability required, with the emphasis on the importance of the job obligations, is the test for application of the "equal responsibility" standard. This test would be met, according to the Wage-Hour Division's interpretative bulletin (FEP 401:483), in such situations as the following:

► If one in a group of employees is required to assume supervisory responsibilities in the absence of a regular supervisor. But minor differences would not justify a pay differential.

► If one sales clerk is designated to determine whether to accept customer's personal checks, there would be a responsibility justifying a differential.

But minor differences, such as the responsibility for turning out the lights or locking up at the end of the day would not justify a differential.

SIMILAR WORKING CONDITIONS

In its interpretative bulletin on the Equal Pay Act, the Wage-Hour Division observes that generally employees performing jobs requiring equal skill, effort, and responsibility are likely to be performing them under similar working conditions. But in situations where some employees performing work meeting the equal skill, effort, and responsibility standards have working conditions substantially different from those required for the performance of other jobs, the equal-pay principle would not apply and a differential would be permissible. (FEP 401:484) In other words, a practical judgment must be made to determine whether differences in working conditions are of the kind to be taken into consideration in setting wage levels.

The mere fact that jobs are in different departments, for example, will not justify a pay differential. But if some employees do the majority of their work outside the establishment, while others do most of their work inside, the working conditions would appear to be dissimilar, permitting a pay differential.

In a case involving a glass company, the Supreme Court held in 1974 that the company violated the Act when it paid men inspectors on the night shift a higher base wage than it paid women inspectors working days and doing the same job.

The pay differential, the Court found, originated at a time when only higher wages could induce men to perform what was termed "women's work."

But the Court pointed out that it was not questioning an employer's right to establish "non-discriminatory" wage differentials for night work as long as they did not operate as "an added payment based on sex." A night-rate differential, of itself, would not violate the Act, since "work on a steady night shift no doubt has psychological and physiological impacts making it less attractive than work on a day shift."

But in this case, the Court concluded, the pay differential "arose simply because men would not work at the low rates paid women inspectors." As such, it violated the Act. (Corning Glass Works v. Brennan, 9 FEP Cases 919)

FACTORS OTHER THAN SEX

Not all differentials in pay as between the sexes are unlawful if the employer can establish that the differential is based on a factor other then sex.

Three specific exceptions are discussed above under the heading "Exceptions." These relate to payments made pursuant to a seniority system, a merit system, or a system measuring earnings by quality or quantity of production.

But as pointed out by the Third Circuit, factors "other than sex" need not be job-related or typically used in setting wage scales.

The court upheld higher pay for salespersons selling men's clothes than to those selling women's clothes. The distinction was based on a greater profitability to the employer. In holding such a differential permissible if based on legitimate business concerns, the court relied in part on the legislative history of the Act. (Hodgson v. Robert Hall Clothes, Inc., 20 WH Cases 1100)

INSURANCE CONTRIBUTIONS

For the purpose of the equal-pay standard, as well as Title VII, contributions made by an employer to pension or welfare plans are considered "wages." If the employer makes no contributions to a plan, differences in benefits will not be regarded as a violation. But if a contribution is made, one of these two tests must be met to be in compliance.

► Benefits paid to men and women performing equal work must be equal; *or*

► Contributions by the employer or costs to the employer for men and women performing equal work must be equal. (FEP 421:307)

So if either the benefits or the employer contributions or costs are equal, there is no violation of the equal-pay standard.

This differs from the interpretation adopted by the EEOC under Title VII. EEOC takes the position that all aspects of an insurance, pension, profit-sharing, or other fringe benefit plan must be equal without regard to sex. (See above under "Sex Discrimination: Insurance, Pension Benefits" for a discussion of EEOC's interpretation.)

Hospital Benefits. If an employer offers family hospital coverage to men, but requires women to pay the difference between individual and family coverage, there would be a violation of the equal-pay standard. (Wage-Hour Opinion Letter, February 11, 1966)

Maternity Benefits. Maternity benefits are not regarded as "wages" under the equal-pay standard. Since they do not constitute remuneration for employment, they are beyond the scope of the

Act. (Wage-Hour Opinion Letter, January 7, 1966) But the EEOC has taken the position that maternity coverage falls within Title VII. (See FEP 421:601.)

The question of whether pregnancy is a disability under state laws and collective bargaining contracts is discussed above under "Sex Discrimination: Pregnancy as Disability."

TRAINING PROGRAMS

The absence of a bona fide training program has caused several courts to reject the contention that men could be paid more than women in equal jobs because the men were management trainees. (Hodgson v. Security National Bank, 20 WH Cases 653; Hodgson v. Behren's Drug Co., 9 FEP Cases 816)

In the Behren's case, the court suggested that absence of participation by women in the alleged management training program would be reason for the court to examine the program carefully.

ELIMINATING DIFFERENTIALS

If wage differentials based on sex exist, they must be eliminated under the equal-pay standard by raising the pay of the lower paid employees, instead of reducing the pay of the higher paid employees. The Act specifically provided that compliance shall not be achieved by reducing the wage of any employee.

Moreover, opening up to women a category of higher paying jobs previously closed to them does not remedy an existing equal-pay discrimination. In so ruling, the Supreme Court stated: "The whole purpose of the Act was to require that these depressed wages be raised." (Corning Glass Works v. Brennan, 9 FEP Cases 919)

UNION OBLIGATIONS

The obligation of carrying out the terms of the Act falls upon unions as well as employers regarding the duty of unions, the Wage-Hour Division has said:

► No union "shall cause or attempt to cause an employer to discriminate against an employee" in violation of the Act. (Wage-Hour Opinion Letter, March 6, 1970)

► Collective bargaining agreements must conform with the equal-pay standard. (Wage-Hour Opinion Letter, March 6, 1970)

► The legistlative intent was that "elimination of wage rate differentials based on sex" is the joint responsibility of the employer and the union. (Wage-Hour Opinion Letter, July 1, 1971)

STATE LAWS

There are equal-pay laws in 37 of the states. The U.S. Act provides that where both the federal and state laws apply the federal equal-pay standard is controlling. But it adds that this will not excuse noncompliance with any other state or other law establishing standards higher than those provided by federal law.

Some state overtime laws require that women be paid overtime rates for work in excess of a specific number of hours in a workweek or workday. To comply with the Act, the employer must pay men who perform equal work in the same establishment the same overtime premium when they work such excess hours.

Although the use of different methods to compute overtime pay for men and women would not, in itself, be a violation of the equal-pay standard, the Division has stated that the results of such computation must in the end provide equal pay for equal work. (Wage-Hour Opinion Letter, December 14, 1964)

RELATIONSHIP TO TITLE VII

In banning job discrimination based on sex, Title VII also provides that its provisions must be "harmonized" with the Equal Pay Act. To avoid conflicting interpretations, the EEOC is supposed to make relevant interpretations and opinions of the Wage-Hour Division applicable to equal-pay complaints filed under Title VII.

The EEOC also has promised to consult with the Wage-Hour Division before issuing an opinion on any matter covered by both Title VII and the Equal Pay Act. (See FEP 401:29.) But there have been conflicting interpretations, such as on pension and welfare plans and testing, as discussed above.

There also have been some disagreements among the courts on the interrelationship between Title VII and the Equal Pay Act. One appeals court, the Fifth Circuit, held that the Equal Pay Act did not require equal pay for a male job and a female job that were in fact not equal, despite the fact that the employer did violate Title VII by reserving the higher paid job for men. (Hodgson v. Brookhaven General Hospital, 9 FEP Cases 579)

But the Third Circuit held that equal pay was required, even though the male and female jobs were in fact unequal where reservation of the higher job for men violated Title VII. (Shultz v. Wheaton Glass Co., 9 FEP Cases 502)

Under the Bennett Amendment to Title VII, an employer does not violate Title VII if a disparity in payment is lawful under the Equal Pay Act. Accordingly, a federal district court threw out a challenge under Title VII by female employees against an employer that paid men more for allegedly comparable, but concededly unequal, work. (IUE v. Westinghouse Electric Corp., DC, W VA, 17 FEP Cases 16)

The D.C. Circuit held that an employer was liable under both Title VII and the Equal Pay Act where men and women whose jobs were essentially equal were paid at different rates. The case involved airline stewardesses and pursers, and the court rejected the company's contention that if the stewardess job and the purser job are equal under the Equal Pay Act, there can be no violation of Title VII for barring women from seeking the purser jobs. (Laffey v. Northwest Airlines, 13 FEP Cases 1068)

DISCRIMINATION BY LABOR UNIONS

OBLIGATIONS OF UNIONS

The obligations imposed on labor organizations by Title VII have two aspects. First, where a union acts as an employer, it has the same duty as any other employer not to discriminate in employment on the basis of race, color, religion, sex, national origin, or age.

Second, in its capacity as a union, it may not do any of the following:

► Exclude or expel from membership or otherwise discriminate against a person because of his race, color, religion, sex, national origin, or age.

► Limit, segregate, or classify membership and membership applicants or fail or refuse to refer an individual for employment in any way that would deprive or tend to deprive him of employment opportunities or would limit such employment opportunities or otherwise adversely affect his status as an employee or applicant for employment because of his race, color, religion, sex, national origin, or age.

► Cause or attempt to cause an employer to discriminate against an individual because of his race, color, religion, sex, national origin, or age.

► Operate or join with employers in the operation of an apprenticeship training or retraining program in which discrimination is practiced on the basis of race, color, religion, sex, national origin, or age.

NONDISCRIMINATION CLAUSE

Under the policies of the EEOC, a union has a duty not only to refrain from engaging in discriminatory practices of its own but also of challenging discriminatory practices of employers with whom the union bargains.

This becomes particularly important, where there is no non-discrimination clause in the collective bargaining contract or where the contract has a seniority clause found to have a discriminatory effect. In such a case, the union and the employer may be held jointly liable for back pay to the employees against whom there was unlawful discrimination.

If a union *has* a nondiscrimination clause in its contract, its failure to use it for protesting discriminatory practices of the employer may be considered a violation of Title VII by EEOC. (EEOC Decision, July 15, 1970, Decision No. 71-27; 2 FEP Cases 867)

Moreover, a union's failure to propose a nondiscrimination clause in its contract may be considered a violation by EEOC. A failure to process grievances of black members who alleged discrimination was considered not to be justified by the absence of a nondiscrimination clause in the union's contract. (EEOC Sixth Annual Report, Decision No. 71-90)

Along the same lines, a union's failure to propose an alternative to a seniority system that perpetuated the effects of past unlawful discrimination was considered by the EEOC to be a violation of Title VII, as also was a refusal to publish the collective bargaining agreement in Spanish where a substantial number of the employees spoke and read only Spanish. (EEOC Decision, Nov. 16, 1970, Decision No. 71-48; 3 FEP Cases 97; EEOC Sixth Annual Report, Decision No. 71-2029)

SENIORITY SYSTEMS

Where a collective bargaining contract contains a seniority system both the company and the union may be held liable if the seniority system is found to violate Title VII.

This issue has been extensively litigated, with varying results. But in 1977, the Supreme Court handed down two landmark decisions that modified or overturned many of the lower court decisions.

A key to both decisions was Section 703(h), which provides an exemption for bona fide seniority systems. The fact that a seniority system perpetuated pre-Act discrimination, even post-Act discrimination, the Court said, does not affect its bona fide status. Section 703(h) immunizes all bona fide seniority systems. The key to whether a system is bona fide is whether it was adopted without a discriminatory motive. If so, it is insulated from attack by Section 703(h). The case was Teamsters v. U.S. (T.I.M.E.-D.C. Inc.), 14 FEP Cases 1514.

In the second case, an employee who was discharged and later rehired, sued to obtain seniority back to the date of her original employment. Then seniority system based seniority solely on current employment. Nevertheless, the Supreme Court said, the seniority system was bona fide and insulated from attack by Section 703(h). The case was United Airlines v. Evans, 14 FEP Cases 1510.

Both the Teamsters and United Airlines cases and their background are discussed in detail above under "Discrimination by Employers on the Basis of Race: Seniority Systems." This is followed by a discussion of the "last hired, first fired" policy under collective bargaining contracts.

ADMISSION STANDARDS

As a general rule, the courts have held that union admission standards that operate in a manner that unnecessarily disqualifies individuals for membership on the basis of race, color, sex, national origin, or age are unlawful. In the early years of the 1964 Act, courts made these rulings:

► A local union was found to have engaged in a "pattern or practice" of discrimination against blacks and Mexican Americans by maintaining membership rules that required that a new member be related to a present member, recommended by a member of the local, and approved by a majority vote. The local was ordered by the Fifth Circuit to suspend the membership standards, admit four complainants, and refer nine others for immediate employment. (Vogler v. McCarthy, Inc., 1 FEP Cases 197, 577)

► Two local unions were found to be carrying on the effects of past discrimination with respect to apprenticeship, membership, and job referral, despite the fact that their policy had changed to include blacks after the adoption of Title VII. The unions were ordered by the Eighth Circuit to modify the experience requirements for blacks, as well as the journeyman's examination, and to give those blacks beyond the apprenticeship age the opportunity to take the journeyman's test. (U.S. v. Local 36, Sheet Metal Workers and Local 1, Electrical Workers [IBEW], 2 FEP Cases 127)

Applicants for Union Membership. Although the Civil Rights Act of 1964 did not cover applicants for union membership, the 1972 amendments made it clear that it shall be an unlawful employment practice for a union to limit, segregate, or classify its membership or applicants for membership. This amendment was intended to be merely declaratory of preexisting law as reflected in decisions of the courts, including the decision of the Supreme Court in Phillips v. Martin Marietta Corp. (3 FEP Cases 40)

UNION REFERRAL SYSTEMS

If a union in the past operated a hiring hall on a discriminatory basis, a referral system that gave credit for experience gained under the old system has been regarded by the courts as a violation of Title VII.

A union with a disproportionately low membership of women was found to violate Title VII by the Ninth Circuit when it made and enforced a collective bargaining contract requiring studios in the stage and motion picture industry to give preference to union members on an industry experience roster. Because the roster rarely was exhausted, women were unable to gain the experience necessary for membership in the union and placement on the roster. (Kaplan v. IATSE, 11 FEP Cases 872)

FAIR REPRESENTATION

Under the Taft-Hartley Act, the Railway Labor Act, and Title VII, a union that is an exclusive bargaining representative has an obligation to represent all members of the bargaining unit fairly and on a nondiscriminatory basis. In the leading case of Vaca v. Sipes, the Supreme Court held that if a union's actions are "arbitrary, discriminatory, or in bad faith," they may amount to unfair representation. Moreover, negligence of a union in processing a grievance may provide a basis for a finding of a breach of fair representation. (64 LRRM 2369)

The Supreme Court added to this doctrine in a later case involving the discharge of a group of employees for dishonesty. The union carried the case through the grievance-arbitration procedure under the contract, and the arbitrator denied the grievance. Later, evidence was discovered that showed that the charges against the grievants were not true. But the union did no more, and lower courts refused to upset the arbitration decision, stating that the contract contained a provision that an arbitration award would be "final and binding," and it would impair the arbitration process to permit the issue to be relitigated.

The Supreme Court disagreed. Where the contractual processes have been flawed by the union's failure to represent employees honestly, in good faith, and without invidious discrimination or arbitrary conduct, the Court said, the employees may sue on their own with their own counsel under Section 301 of the Taft-Hartley Act. (Hines v. Anchor Motor Freight, Inc., 91 LRRM 2481)

BYPASSING UNION

If a group of minority employees bypass their collective bargaining representative and act on their own to eliminate discrimination, they may lose their protection under the Taft-Hartley Act.

In a case involving a San Francisco department store, two black employees picketed the store and distributed handbills to protest the alleged racial discrimination by the employer. They were discharged.

At the time the employees picketed, the union representing them was pursuing a grievance involving the alleged racial discrimination. The Supreme Court held that by acting in derogation of their collective bargaining representative the employees lost their protection under the Taft-Hartley Act, and so the employer lawfully could discharge them. (Emporium Capwell Co. v. WACO, 9 FEP Cases 195)

MERGER OF SEGREGATED LOCALS

Early in the history of Title VII, the courts made clear that local unions which segregated on the basis of race would not be tolerated.

In one of the first cases involving the issue, the Fifth Circuit ordered the merger of two segregated locals at the Jacksonville Terminal Company. The action was a "pattern-or-practice" suit brought by the Justice Department. (3 FEP Cases 862)

The same court went even further in a later case. Although refusing to hold all segregation of local unions to be a *per se* violation of Title VII, the court ruled that once a district court finds that actual discrimination in employment results from segregation of locals, it has no discretion to refuse to order that the locals be merged. (EEOC v. Longshoremen, 10 FEP Cases 545)

REMEDIES FOR UNION DISCRIMINATION

The courts prescribed a variety of remedies in cases in which unions have engaged in or caused discrimination. The remedies include affirmative action.

In one case, for example, a construction union was found to have engaged in discrimination by failing to admit nonwhites to full journeyman status, discriminating against them in work referral, and participating in a discriminatory apprenticeship program.

The Second Circuit ordered the union to adopt an affirmative action program to bring nonwhite participation in the union to a set percentage. The court said that the program was not barred by the preference or quota provision of Title VII. That provision, it added, prohibits only quota hiring used to remedy racial imbalance not caused by unlawful discrimination. (Rios v. Steamfitters, 8 FEP Cases 293)

DISCRIMINATION BY EMPLOYMENT AGENCIES

Employment agencies often have a key position in the hiring process. For this reason, they are given specific attention in Title VII and other federal and state laws and orders regulating employment discrimination.

Under Title VII, it is an unlawful employment practice for an employment agency:

► To fail or refuse to refer for employment or otherwise to discriminate against any person because of his race, color, religion, sex, or national origin.

► To classify or refer any person for employment on the basis of his race, color, religion, sex, or national origin.

These prohibitions apply not only to private employment agencies, but also to the United States Employment Service and state and local employment services that receive federal assistance.

Most of the restrictions discussed above under "Discrimination by Employers" also apply to employment agencies. This includes unlawful preemployment inquiries as specified under federal and state regulations.

The list of unlawful preemployment questions adopted under the New York Act was upheld by the New York Court of Appeals in Holland v. Edwards. The court found that the job applicant was questioned about her change of name and her national origin, as reflected by her name and schooling, the religion of one of her former employers, and the maiden name of her former employer's wife. (1 FEP Cases 9)

EEOC also has held that a requirement that a photograph accompany an employment application may be regarded as evidence of discrimination.

Most employment agency cases have involved alleged violations of the Age Discrimination Act. For example, the Fourth Circuit held that an agency's ads addressed to "recent college graduates" do not automatically violate the Act. When the ads are part of a general invitation to a specific class of prospective customers coming into the job market at a particular time of the year to use the agency's services, the Act is not violated. However, if used in reference to a specific job opportunity, use of the phrase violates the Act because it implies that older persons need not apply.

Contrary to the Labor Department's position, the court held that "trigger words" such as "returning veterans" and "recent college grad" are not discriminatory per se. The effect is determined by context rather than words. (Hodgson v. Approved Personnel Services, 11 FEP Cases 688)

Disparate Treatment in Own Operations. An employment agency also may violate Title VII by the way it handles its own operations.

It may not, for example, designate applicant stations as "male" and "female," or have counselors work exclusively with referrals for one sex. (See EEOC Decision, July 20, 1971, 4 FEP Cases 254.)

EXECUTIVE ORDERS ON AFFIRMATIVE ACTION

Employers who do business with the Government have an obligation to refrain from employment discrimination that goes beyond that imposed by Title VII. The significant differences are:

► Unlike Title VII, the executive orders require that contractors take affirmative action to ensure equal employment opportunity. There is no prohibition against "preferential" or "quota" hiring.

► The orders declare a policy against employment discrimination based on age or physical handicap, in addition to race, color, religion, sex, or national origin.

ORDERS, LAWS INVOLVED

► Executive Order 11246 (FEP 401:601) covers discrimination based on race, color, religion, sex, or national origin. Executive Order 11141 covers discrimination based on age. (FEP 401:615)

The orders are complemented by Section 503 of the Rehabilitation Act of 1973 (FEP 401:501), requiring affirmative action and reasonable accommodation in hiring qualified physically and mentally handicapped persons; and Section 2012 of the Vietnam Era Veterans Readjustment Assistance Act of 1974, calling for affirmative action in hiring and promoting Vietnam era and all disabled veterans. (FEP 401:521)

WHO IS COVERED

Executive Order 11246 covers all government contractors except those exempted by the Secretary of Labor. The Secretary has exempted companies whose amount of business with the Government does not exceed $10,000 a year. Apart from this the exemption power has been used sparingly.

Moreover, a federal district court has held that a company need not enter into any formal contract with the Government to be considered a contractor under Executive Order 11246. As long as a company supplies a service to a government agency and receives payment from the agency in excess of $10,000 a year, the company is a contractor subject to the order. (U.S. v. New Orleans Public Service, Inc., 8 FEP Cases 1089) On appeal, the Fifth Circuit held that E.O. 11246 has the force and effect of law and that the non-discrimination clause is imposed on employers holding government contracts regardless of whether the employers expressly have consented to that clause and regardless of whether the clause is physically incorporated in the contract. (14 FEP Cases 1735)

WHAT ORDERS REQUIRE

A contractor covered by the orders must meet these requirements:

► Refrain from discriminating against any employee or job applicant because of race, color, religion, sex, or national origin.

► Take affirmative action to ensure that applicants are employed and employees are treated without regard to race, color, religion, sex, or national origin. The obligation extends to working conditions and facilities, such as rest rooms, as well as to hiring, firing, layoff and recall, promotions, compensation, and so forth.

► State in all advertisements or help solicitations that all qualified applicants will receive consideration without regard to race, color, religion, sex, or national origin.

► Advise each labor union with which the contractor deals of its commitments under the order.

► Include the obligation under the order in every subcontract or purchase order unless specifically exempted.

► Comply with all provisions of the order and the rules and regulations; furnish all information and reports required; permit access to books, records, and accounts for the purpose of investigation to ascertain compliance.

► File regular compliance reports describing hiring and employment practices.

AFFIRMATIVE ACTION

Under Order No. 4, issued by the Office of Federal Contract Compliance Programs, government contractors are required to develop affirmative action plans containing the following:

► An analysis of all major job classifications, with an explanation of any "under utilization" of minorities in any of the job classes.

► Goals and targets and affirmative action commitments designed to relieve any deficiencies. But the order specifies that a contractor's compliance will not be judged solely by whether he reaches his goals and meets his timetables.

► Instead, a contractor's compliance will be reviewed and determined by reviewing the contents of his program, the extent of his adherence to it, and his good-faith efforts to make his program work toward realization of the goals within timetables set for completion.

The guidelines under Order No. 4 also outline suggested procedures for use in establishing, implementing, and judging an acceptable affirmative action program. The contractor must consider such factors as these:

► The minority population of the labor area surrounding the facility and the size of the minority unemployment force.

► The general availability of minorities having requisite skills in the immediate labor area and in an area in which the contractor can reasonably recruit.

► The availability of promotable minority employees within the contractor's organization.

► The anticipated expansion, contraction, and turnover in the labor force.

► The existence of training institutions capable of training minorities in the requisite skills.

► The degree of training which the contractor is reasonably able to undertake as a means of making all job classes available to minorities.

There also are sex guidelines. These are negative in nature—specifying what a contractor may *not* do, such as making a distinction based on sex in advertising for jobs; making a distinction based on sex in employment opportunities; relying on state protective laws to justify denying a job to a woman; denying a job to a woman with children.

COMPLIANCE PROCEDURES

To guide the procurement agencies in reviewing affirmative action programs of government contractors, the OFCCP issued

Revised Order No. 14. The order provides for a compliance review of nonconstruction contractors or subcontractors with 50 or more employees and a contract of more than $50,000.

Under Executive Order 11246, such contractors must develop written action programs that "must relate to all major job categories at the facility with explanations if minorities or women are currently being under-utilized." Where there are deficiencies, goals and timetables are required to utilize minorities and women at all levels and in all segments of the work force.

Compliance review is undertaken in a series of steps. The procedure is as follows:

► First, the contractor receives a request from OFCCP for a copy of the affirmative action plan to be forwarded to the compliance officer.

► If the compliance officer determines that the affirmative action program is inadequate, he may conduct an on-site inspection of the plant. He is not required to notify the contractor of the date of the inspection.

► During an on-site review, the compliance officer may ask such questions as how has the contractor sought to establish his EEO image in the community, does he use institutional as well as recruitment advertising, is an EEO reference included in advertising, and are lower level supervisors disseminating the EEO policy?

SENIORITY

Unlike Title VII, the executive order does not contain any provision excepting conduct taken pursuant to a bona fide seniority system. Does this mean that a government contractor may not follow a seniority system that perpetuates the effects of past discrimination, even though Title VII says it can? The Fifth Circuit ruled in the East Texas Motor Freight case (16 FEP Cases 163) that the answer is "no." Because Congress declared in Section 703(h) that a bona fide seniority system is lawful, it said, the executive order may not be interpreted as making such a seniority system unlawful. The court rejected a contention that the obligations on government contractors under the executive order are "above and beyond" those imposed on contractors by Title VII.

BACK PAY, PENALTIES

Enforcement procedures and penalties are more stringent under the executive orders for government contractors than they are for employers generally under Title VII.

An employer found to have violated the orders may be debarred from government contracts. The OFCCP may place the contractor on an ineligible list circulated to the procurement agencies. Moreover, the right of the Government to seek back pay from a contractor charged with discriminatory employment practices under Executive Order 11246 has been upheld. (U.S. v. Duquesne Light Co., 13 FEP Cases 1608)

CONSTRUCTION PLANS

In the construction industry, a nonnegotiable system of goals or quotas was established by the OFCCP for federal construction contractors under so-called hometown plans. In the Philadelphia Plan, the first to be issued, bidders on federal construction contracts exceeding $500,000 were required to specify hiring goals set on the basis of area population prior to the award of the contract.

The goals were aimed at increasing minority-group employment in seven of the higher paying building trades — iron work, plumbing and pipefitting, steamfitting, sheet metal work, electrical work, roofing and elevator construction. Similar hometown plans were imposed or agreed upon voluntarily in over 60 areas.

In the first court test on the legality of such plans, the U.S. Court of Appeals at Philadelphia found no inherent conflict between the quota or preferential hiring prohibition in Title VII and the minority-group hiring goals under construction contracts covered by the Philadelphia Plan. The goals, the court said, were valid executive action to remedy the past exclusion of minority-group workers from such jobs. (Contractors Association of Eastern Pennsylvania v. Shultz, 3 FEP Cases 395)

In 1977, however, the Labor Department decided to eliminate the "imposed" affirmative action plans for Philadelphia, Washington, D.C., San Francisco, St. Louis, Atlanta, and Camden, N.J. Instead, OFCCP will require the inclusion of EEO specifications in basic construction contracts. "Hometown" plans voluntarily established in 42 metropolitan areas were continued in effect.

At the same time, OFCCP proposed affirmative action programs with the goal of increasing the employment of women on federally supported construction projects to 6.9 percent by 1980.

VETERANS' READJUSTMENT ASSISTANCE ACT

The Vietnam Era Veterans Readjustment Assistance Act of 1974 requires employers with government contracts or subcontracts of $10,000 or more to take affirmative action "to employ and advance in employment" disabled veterans and qualified veterans of the Vietnam era. (FEP 401:521)

In addition to the affirmative action requirement, the Act imposes an obligation on all covered employers to list all suitable job openings with the appropriate local employment service. Referral priority then will be given to Vietnam era veterans.

The enforcement of the Act is by complaint. If a person believes he has been discriminated against by a contractor, he may file a complaint with the Veterans' Employment Service of the Department of Labor. The Secretary of Labor is required to take such action as is consistent with the terms of the contract and the laws and regulations.

FEDERAL DISCRIMINATION LAWS: ADMINISTRATION AND ENFORCEMENT

The responsibility for administering and enforcing the federal laws and orders dealing with employment discrimination is spread among a number of agencies and the courts. Moreover, in some instances there is an overlapping of jurisdiction. The administrative agencies involved include:

The Equal Employment Opportunity Commission (EEOC). The five members of the Commission are appointed by the President and confirmed by the Senate. There also is a General Counsel appointed and confirmed in the same way.

Under the 1964 version of Title VII, EEOC was given authority merely to investigate and conciliate charges of unlawful employment discrimination. If it found reasonable cause to believe a violation had been committed, it notified the aggrieved individual or individuals who then could file an action in court.

The 1972 amendments gave EEOC authority to file a court action on its own if it found reasonable cause to believe a violation had been committed and it could not settle it by conference, persuasion, or conciliation.

The Office of Federal Contract Compliance Programs (OFCCP). Established in the Labor Department, OFCCP administers Executive Order No. 11246, which forbids employment discrimination based on race, color, religion, sex or national origin by federal contractors and subcontractors and by contractors performing work under a federally assisted construction contract. There is no number-of-employees standard. Under the Order, contractors and subcontractors bidding on government contracts must submit affirmative action programs to OFCCP to insure equal opportunity in all aspects of employment.

Wage and Hour Division of the Labor Department. The Division is responsible for administering and enforcing both the Equal

Pay Act that forbids discrimination in pay on the basis of sex and the Age Discrimination in Employment Act. As of July 1, 1979, however, these functions will be transferred to the EEOC in the case of both laws.

The U.S. Civil Service Commission. CSC is given authority to enforce Executive Order 11478 requiring equal employment opportunity in the federal service based on merit and fitness and without discrimination based on race, color, religion, sex, or national origin. In addition, Section 717 added to Title VII by the 1972 amendments gives the CSC authority to police such discrimination in the federal service. Although federal employees do not have access to EEOC, they may file an action in a federal district court following CSC procedures and may obtain a trial *de novo*.

The Department of Justice. Prior to 1974, Justice brought pattern-or-practice actions under Title VII, but this jurisdiction was transferred to the EEOC. But the Justice Department still enforces Tile VII in cases involving a state or local governmental agency or political subdivision.

The National Labor Relations Board. Although not directly involved in policing discrimination based on race, religion, sex, or national origin, the NLRB has become involved in this area under the doctrine of fair representation. Under this doctrine, a union that is an exclusive collective bargaining representative has a duty to represent employees in the bargaining unit fairly and without invidious discrimination. This includes discrimination based on race.

For about three years, the NLRB followed a policy of refusing to certify a union as a bargaining representative, even though it had won an election, if it was established that the union engaged in invidious discrimination against some members of the bargaining unit. But in 1977, the Board overturned this policy, holding that a claim that a union engages in invidious discrimination may not be raised to bar the union's certification as a bargaining representative. The only appropriate vehicle for resolving such issues and devising appropriate remedies, including the revocation of certification, the Board said, is an unfair labor practice proceeding. (Handy Andy, Inc., 94 LRRM 1354)

Prior to this decision, the Board refused to hold sex discrimination by an employer a violation of the Taft-Hartley Act, pointing out that such matters may be remedied under Title VII of the Civil

Rights Act and other related laws and orders. (Jubilee Manufacturing Co., 82 LRRM 1482)

Contracting Agencies. Under Executive Order 11246, contracting agencies and departments cooperate in enforcing equal employment opportunity on government contract work. The agencies and departments also police employment discrimination under any federally assisted program or contract.

EEOC PROCEEDINGS

There are two methods for instituting an administrative proceeding before the EEOC.

▶ First, a charge may be filed in writing and under oath by or on behalf of a person claiming to be aggrieved.

▶ Second, a written charge may be filed by a member of the Commission who has reasonable cause to believe that a violation has occurred. Such a charge also must be sworn to.

About half of the states and some 70 municipalities have laws or ordinances forbidding discrimination in employment for the reasons specified in Title VII.

To give the state and local agencies the first opportunity to resolve some of the issues involving alleged discrimination, Title VII provides that no charge may be filed with the EEOC by an aggrieved person before the expiration of 60 days after proceedings have been started under state or local law or after termination of such proceedings, whichever occurs first. If a state or municipality has a new law, the EEOC deferral period is extended to 120 days.

The purpose of this deferral policy was to support and encourage the operation of the state agencies. It was not intended to complicate the filing of complaints Although Title VII states that no charge may be filed with EEOC without first going to the state or local agency, the Supreme Court has approved EEOC's practice of accepting a charge, orally referring it to the state or local agency on behalf of the charging party, and then beginning to process it upon the expiration of the deferral period without requiring the filing of a new charge. (Love v. Pullman Co., 4 FEP Cases 150)

The 1972 amendments require EEOC to accord "substantial weight" to the final findings and orders by state and local agencies. But EEOC will designate as appropriate deferral agencies only those whose laws prohibit essentially all the practices prohibited by Title VII, by essentially all of the persons by whom such practices are illegal under Title VII, and on essentially all the grounds covered by Title VII.

PROCESSING A CHARGE

As amended in 1972, Title VII sets out the following steps for processing a charge of unlawful employment discrimination:

► A charge must be filed within 180 days after the alleged unlawful employment practice. If a charge is filed initially with a state or local agency within 180 days after the alleged unlawful practice occurred, the charge then must be filed with the EEOC within 300 days after the alleged practice occurred or within 30 days after receiving notice that the state or local agency has ended its proceedings, whichever occurs first.

► After a charge is filed, or the state or local deferral is ended, EEOC must serve a notice of the charge on the respondent within 10 days.

► EEOC then must investigate the charge to determine whether there is reasonable cause to believe that the charge is true. The determination of reasonable cause must be made as promptly as possible and, so far as practicable, within 120 days.

► If it finds no reasonable cause, the EEOC must dismiss the charge; if it finds reasonable cause, it must attempt to conciliate.

► If the EEOC is unable to obtain an acceptable conciliation agreement within 30 days, it may bring a civil action in a federal district court.

► If the EEOC doesn't bring an action within 180 days, it then must notify the aggrieved party, who then has 90 days to file a suit on his own behalf.

Before the 1972 amendments to Title VII, a number of court decisions permitted aggrieved persons to sue before EEOC completed the required procedural steps. The courts reasoned that the individuals should not be penalized by the delays of EEOC.

In contrast, EEOC itself has been strictly required to go through all the procedures specified by the Act before filing a suit on its own. Moreover, failure by EEOC to follow its own regulations for initiating suits may provide ground for dismissal of an action. In one case, for example, the Eighth Circuit Court of Appeals upheld the dismissal of a case where EEOC failed to follow its regulation requiring it to give notice of termination of conciliation efforts to an employer who had refused to participate in the proceeding. The court stressed the importance of conciliation under Title VII. (EEOC v. Hickey-Mitchell Co., 8 FEP Cases 1281)

CONCILIATION PROCEEDINGS

Under both Title VII and the Age Discrimination in Employment Act, special emphasis is placed on conciliation of charges of discrimination.

Title VII allows 30 days for the EEOC to work out a conciliation agreement between the parties before a suit may be brought. Nothing said or done during the attempt to achieve voluntary compliance may be made public without the written consent of the parties. Nor may it be used in a subsequent court action. The conciliation procedure is as follows:

► After the Commission decides that there is cause to believe that discrimination has occurred, the Director of Compliance notifies the charging party and the respondent that a conciliator will contact them to resolve the dispute.

► The conciliator first meets with the charging party to determine what remedy would be satisfactory. He then tries to persuade the respondent to accept a remedy acceptable to the charging party and the EEOC.

► If accepted by the respondents, the remedy is embodied in a conciliation agreement that is signed by the charging party and the respondent and submitted to EEOC for approval.

► If the respondent fails or refuses to conciliate or to make a good-faith effort to resolve the dispute, EEOC may terminate its conciliation efforts and so notify the respondent. Conciliation efforts will not be resumed except upon a written request from the respondent within a specified period.

► If the EEOC terminates the conciliation procedure without providing the notification called for by its regulations, a subsequent suit by EEOC against the employer may be subject to dismissal. (See EEOC v. Hickey-Mitchell Co., 8 FEP Cases 1281.)

► In addition to remedying the charging party's individual complaint, EEOC normally attempts to include in the conciliation agreement modifications of other employment practices to bring them into compliance with Title VII. This could include an affirmative action program.

SETTLEMENT AGREEMENTS

To avoid lengthy and costly court enforcement or contract debarment proceedings, EEOC and OFCCP have coordinated their efforts to negotiate settlement agreements with major companies and industries. The Justice Department has also participated in some of the negotiations.

The first settlement agreement was reached in January 1973 with the American Telephone and Telegraph Company and its 24 operating companies. Without admitting any violations, the companies agreed to pay about $15 million to 13,000 women and 2,000 men who were members of minority groups who had been denied pay and promotion opportunities.

In addition, the companies agreed to develop goals for increasing the utilization of women and minorities in each job classification of all 700 establishments within the Bell System.

A second settlement of national significance was reached the following year between the Government — EEOC and Justice — and nine major steel companies and the United Steelworkers Union. In addition to providing back pay for 40,000 employees, the agreement set goals and timetables for filling openings in trade and craft jobs with women and minority group employees. The settlement was upheld by the Fifth Circuit Court of Appeals. (U.S. v. Allegheny-Ludlum Industries, 11 FEP Cases 167)

COURT PROCEEDINGS

Before the 1972 amendments, enforcement of Title VII was left primarily to private suits by aggrieved individuals. The role of EEOC was confined to the informal methods of conference, conciliation, and persuasion.

The amendments gave EEOC authority to bring court actions. If it is unable to obtain an acceptable conciliation agreement within 30 days after the filing of the charge or the expiration of the state agency deferral period, EEOC may bring an action against the respondent in a federal district court. Where a state or local government is the respondent, the action is brought by the Justice Department. The aggrieved individual retains the right to bring an action on his own if he is dissatisfied with the Government's handling of the case.

What if EEOC brings a suit where a suit based on the same charge already has been brought by an individual? The federal appeals courts have disagreed on EEOC's right to maintain an action under such circumstances.

The Eighth Circuit, for example, has held that where EEOC has failed to obtain conciliation of a charge filed by an individual, notifies him of his right to sue, and he sues within the required statutory period, EEOC may not later bring a separate suit based on the same charge. There is only a right of intervention. The aggrieved individual has an absolute right to intervene if EEOC has filed a suit. EEOC has a permissive right to intervene if the charging party has brought an action. (EEOC v. Missouri Pacific R.R. Co., 7 FEP Cases 177)

The Ninth Circuit similarly reasoned that EEOC apparently is restricted to an intervenor's status once a private action has been filed. (EEOC v. Occidental Life Insurance Co., 12 FEP Cases 1300)

But the Third Circuit adopted a different view. It decided that EEOC has the power to bring a civil suit, and it does not lose that power when a private party brings a suit based on the same facts. (EEOC v. North Hills Passavant Hospital, 13 FEP Cases 1129)

UNIONS, OTHER ORGANIZATIONS

The standing of unions, ethnic groups, and other organizations to bring suits under Title VII has received mixed treatment in the courts. With respect to unions, for example, it has been held:

► A union has standing to bring a Title VII suit. (Thompson v. Board of Education, 12 FEP Cases 1700)

► A union lacked adequacy of representation in a class action. (Social Services Union v. County of Santa Clara, 12 FEP Cases 570)

► Unions are indispensable parties under Rule 19 of the Federal Rules of Civil Procedure. (EEOC v. McLean Trucking Co., 11 FEP Cases 833)

► On the other hand, unions are merely proper parties. (U.S. v. Navaho Freight Lines, Inc., 11 FEP Cases 787)

► A police officers' association was recognized as having standing to sue. (Chicano Police Officers' Ass'n v. Stover, 11 FEP Cases 1056) Also see League of United Latin American Citizens v. City of Santa Ana, 11 FEP Cases 815. But a standing to sue was not recognized in Urban Contractors Alliance v. Bi-State Development Agency, 12 FEP Cases 1285.

INDIVIDUAL ACTIONS

As mentioned above, an aggrieved individual has the right to seek his own court remedy where he takes the view that the EEOC has not pursued his complaint speedily enough or has entered into an unsatisfactory agreement with the respondent.

In such a case the courts may, at the grievant's request, appoint an attorney to represent him and to begin the action without payment of fees. EEOC or the Attorney General may intervene in the action if it is certified that the action is of general public importance.

These individual actions raise a number of critical questions. Some have been answered; others have not.

Must the individual first have filed a charge with EEOC? Must he wait until EEOC makes an attempt at conciliation? Must he also wait until EEOC has found reasonable cause to believe that his charge has merit?

Apart from the need to pursue his remedies before EEOC, is the individual required to pursue any available remedies under an applicable collective bargaining contract? If he does and loses, may he still sue under Title VII on the same claim?

Here are some of the answers the courts have given:

► The courts have shown reluctance to dismiss a complaint merely because the plaintiff did not proceed properly before EEOC. They also have hesitated to penalize individuals because of delays by the EEOC. (Stebbins v. Nationwide Mutual Insurance Co., 1 FEP Cases 235; Mickel v. South Carolina State Employment Service, 1 FEP Cases 1821) But filing a charge with the EEOC generally is held a prerequisite to a suit.

► Since a plaintiff may represent a class of employees or potential employees who are entitled to relief, the courts may not insist that he have observed all the statutory time limits. (Parham v. Southwestern Bell Telephone Co., 2 FEP Cases 1017) Where systematic discrimination is alleged there may be a continuing violation — one that continues as long as the discriminatory system is in effect. (Robinson v. Lorillard Corp., 3 FEP Cases 653)

► Several appeals courts have held that conciliation efforts by EEOC are not a jurisdictional prerequisite to the bringing of a Title VII suit by an individual. It is merely required that EEOC have an opportunity to persuade the employer or union before the action may be brought. (Gaston County Dyeing Machine Co. v.

Brown, 1 FEP Cases 699; IBEW v. EEOC, 1 FEP Cases 335; Dent v. St. Louis-San Francisco Ry., 1 FEP Cases 583; Choate v. Caterpillar Tractor Co., 1 FEP Cases 431) Several cases so holding were denied review by the Supreme Court.

► Moreover, the Supreme Court has held that the absence of a finding by EEOC of "reasonable cause" to believe a violation has occurred does not bar a suit by an aggrieved individual. He satisfies the jurisdictional requirements by filing timely charges with EEOC and by receiving and acting upon EEOC's statutory notice of the right to sue. Title VII does not restrict an individual's right to sue to those charges on which EEOC has made findings of "reasonable cause." (McDonnell Douglas Corp. v. Green, 5 FEP Cases 965)

► An employee who has submitted his grievance to binding arbitration under a collective bargaining contract does not forfeit his right to file a court action under Title VII based on the same complaint. The action under Title VII is not barred, the Supreme Court said, by the doctrine of election of remedies, the doctrine of waiver, or the federal labor policy respecting arbitration. The federal courts are not required to defer to the arbitrator's decision, but instead should consider the employee's claim *de novo*. (Alexander v. Gardner-Denver Co., 7 FEP Cases 81)

► On a related issue, the Supreme Court ruled that an employee's use of the grievance-arbitration procedure does not toll the statutory time limit on the filing of a charge under Title VII. Since the two actions are independent and may be pursued concurrently, the Court said, the grievance-arbitration proceedings do not toll the Title VII limitation period. (Electrical Workers v. Robbins & Myers, Inc., 13 FEP Cases 1813)

CLASS ACTIONS

Class actions under Title VII are governed by Rule 23(a) of the Federal Rules of Civil Procedure. Rule 23(a) specifies that an action may be maintained as a class action only if all of the following requirements are met:

► The class is so numerous that joinder of all parties is impracticable;

► There are questions of law or fact common to the class;

► The claims or defenses of the representative parties are typical of the claims or defenses of the class; *and*

► The representative parties will fairly and adequately protect the interests of the class.

In addition to these four requirements, all of which must be met, Rule 23(b) specifies three more requirements, one of which must be met. They are: (1) Separate action would create a risk of inconsistent adjudications or adjudications that would substantially impair the ability of nonparties to protect their interests. (2) Where injunctive relief is sought, the party opposing the class has acted or refused to act on grounds generally applicable to the class. *Or* (3) questions of law or fact common to members of the class predominate over questions affecting only individual members, and class action is the superior method for fairly and efficiently adjudicating the controversy.

The federal appeals courts generally have accorded a liberal interpretation to Rules 23(a) and (b). The Seventh Circuit, for example, said: "A suit for violation of Title VII is necessarily a class action as the evil sought to be ended is discrimination on the basis of a class characteristic." (Bowe v. Colgate-Palmolive Co., 2 FEP Cases 121)

Similarly, the Ninth Circuit said that employment discrimination based on race, sex, or national origin is by definition a class action. So Rule 23 must be interpreted liberally not to undermine the purpose and effectiveness of Title VII in eradicating class-based discrimination. (Gay v. Waiters Union, Local 30, 14 FEP Cases 995)

Other courts, however, have scrutinized the action carefully to see that each of the Rule 23 requirements is met. On the requirement that the members of the class are so numerous that joinder is impossible, the courts have not set any specific number of employees required.

The requirement of common questions of law or fact generally has not been an obstacle to plaintiffs seeking a class action. The cases more often have centered on the requirement that claims be typical of the class.

The Tenth Circuit has interpreted this to mean that the persons seeking to bring a class action must establish that there is in fact a class needing representation. They must show, not merely allege, that members of the class are victims of discrimination.

On this basis a suit by a warehouse employee was limited to the class of black employees at the warehouse. The court found that he did not prove that the discriminatory practices existed at other facilities of the employer. (Taylor v. Safeway Stores, Inc., 11 FEP Cases 449)

In determining whether a plaintiff will fairly and adequately represent the class, the major issue generally is whether the plaintiff's interest conflicts with those of class members. In a case involving several airlines, for example, the Stewards and Stewardesses Union was held not to be an adequate representative of former stewards and stewardesses protesting a policy of terminating pregnant stewardesses. So the union was not permitted to settle a class action brought against the airlines by present and former stewardesses. The decision was by the Seventh Circuit. (Stewards v. American Airlines, 6 FEP Cases 1197)

The Fifth Circuit, on the other hand, held that a plaintiff could not be found to be unable to represent a class adequately solely because he is unlikely to prevail on his individual claim. (Huff v. Cass Co., 6 FEP Cases 400)

In another stewardess case, the Seventh Circuit granted class relief to all stewardesses who had been terminated under a no-marriage rule found to be illegal. The court said that class relief could be granted even if the suit was not pleaded as a class action. (Sprogis v. United Airlines, Inc., 4 FEP Cases 37) But the Fifth Circuit held that if a case was not pleaded as a class action, the plaintiff could not obtain class relief. (Danner v. Phillips Petroleum Co., 3 FEP Cases 858)

There also have been some conflicting and confusing holdings on who may be represented and obtain relief in a class action. Some of the major holdings are:

► Each member of the class need not file a charge with the EEOC. A plaintiff may bring a class action on behalf of those who have not filed charges. Moreover, employees who have not filed charges may share in a remedial order of back pay (Albemarle Paper Co. v. Moody, 10 FEP Cases 1181), even if they intervene in an action that is subsequently denied class action status. (Wheeler v. American Home Products Corp., 16 FEP Cases 157)

► Although bringing the action tolls the statute of limitations for all members of the class, a plaintiff may not represent in a class action those who, because of the time limit, could not have filed a charge with EEOC at the time the plaintiff filed charges. (Wetzel v. Liberty Mutual Insurance Co., 9 FEP Cases 209)

► Where the class action is under Title VII exclusively, the Fifth Circuit held, the participation in the suit by members of the class is limited to the issues raised by the employees who did file a charge with the EEOC — or like issues. (Oatis v. Crown Zellerbach Corp., 1 FEP Cases 328) But this would not be true, the Fifth Circuit held later, where the action is filed under both Title VII and the Civil Rights Act of 1866, since they provide independent remedies. (Alpha Portland Cement Co. v. Reese, 10 FEP Cases 126)

PATTERN-OR-PRACTICE CASES

Under the 1964 Civil Rights Act, the Attorney General was given authority to seek an injunction where he had "reasonable cause" to believe that individuals were engaged in a "pattern or practice of resistance" to the rights protected by Title VII. The 1972 amendments transferred this jurisdiction to the EEOC, effective two years later.

On certification that the case is of general public importance, the Attorney General may request that a three-judge court be convened. The case must be assigned for a hearing at the earliest practical date and must be expedited in every way. Appeal from the judgment of the three-judge court may be taken directly to the Supreme Court.

If there is no request for a three-judge court, the chief judge of the district is required to designate a judge in the district to hear and determine the case. If no such judge is available, a judge in another district or a circuit judge may be designated. The case must be heard as soon as possible and expedited in every way.

The procedure has been used against both employers and unions. (See "Remedies Under Title VII" for a discussion of the remedies in pattern-or-practice actions.)

PROVING DISCRIMINATION

How does an individual prove that an employer or union unlawfully discriminated against him on the basis of race, color, religion, sex, or national origin? How does an employer or union rebut such a claim?

The initial burden to provide evidence is on the plaintiff. But once he shows a prima facie case, the burden of rebutting the presumption of discrimination shifts to the employer or other respondent. He must show that the action which is the basis of the charge was based on nondiscriminatory reasons. Even if the respondent adduces such evidence, the charging party may reply with the assertion that the reasons stated by the respondent were pretextual and that the underlying reason was discriminatory.

Basic Rules. In a leading case decided in 1973, the Supreme Court held that a black applicant made out a prima facie case of discrimination by showing:

► He was black;

► He applied for a vacant job for which he was qualified;

► He was rejected; *and*

► The employer continued to seek applicants for the job.

In an attempt to rebut the prima facie case, the employer presented evidence of the applicant's participation in an illegal stall-in in front of the plant for which he was arrested and convicted. The Court said this was sufficient rebuttal of the prima facie case.

But the Court did not stop there. The applicant, it added, had the right to show that the reasons for rejection advanced by the employer were pretextual — a "cover-up" for a racially discriminatory decision.

To show the justification advanced by the employer was a pretext, the Court continued, the employee could show (1) that others similarly situated were not refused employment, (2) the employer's treatment of the employee during previous employment, (3) the employer's reaction to the applicant's previous civil rights activity, and (4) the employer's "general policy and practice with respect to minority employment."

Use of Statistics. Regarding point (4), the Court said: "Statistics as to petitioner's employment policy and practice may be helpful to a determination of whether petitioner's refusal to rehire respondent in this case conformed to a general pattern of discrimination against blacks." (McDonnell Douglas Corp. v. Green, 5 FEP Cases 965)

The Supreme Court elaborated on the doctrine in two cases decided in 1977. Although statistics may be used to prove racially discriminatory hiring practices, the Court said in the first case that the employer (a school district) has the right to have recent hiring practices considered to counter the proof of discrimination. An employer who made all its employment decisions in a wholly nondiscriminatory way from the date it became subject to Title VII would not violate the Act even if it formerly had maintained an all-white work force by purposefully excluding blacks.

In reversing the appeals court decision, the Supreme Court said the appeals court "totally disregarded the possibility" that the finding of discrimination might be rebutted by statistics concerning the school district's hiring practices after it was made subject to Title VII by the 1972 amendments. The Court remanded the case for a more refined statistical analysis of the relevant labor market. (Hazelwood School District v. U.S., 15 FEP Cases 1)

The second case is more notable for its discussion of bona fide seniority systems (see "Seniority Systems," pp. 20-22) than for the rulings on proof of violation. But the Court did add the principles on the use of statistics to prove violations. It made these rulings:

► Statistics showing a racial imbalance in the composition of the employer's work force as compared with the composition of the population in the community from which the workers are hired are of probative value in a case alleging racial discrimination. This is true even though Section 703(j) makes clear that Title VII imposes no requirement that the work force mirror general population.

► Without an explanation, it ordinarily is to be expected that nondiscriminatory hiring practices in time will result in a work force more or less representative of racial composition of the community. However, considerations such as the small size of the sample and evidence showing that figures for the general population might not accurately reflect the pool of qualified job applicants also would be relevant. (Teamsters v. U.S. [T.I.M.E.-DC, Inc.], 14 FEP Cases 1514)

REMEDIES UNDER TITLE VII

Remedies available under Title VII are set out in Section 706(g). They include both injunctions and affirmative action. A respondent found to have intentionally engaged in an unlawful employment practice or to be engaging in one may be enjoined and ordered to take such affirmative action as may be appropriate.

Affirmative action may include:

► Reinstatement or hiring of employees, with or without back pay. Back-pay liability shall not accrue from a date more than two years prior to the filing of a charge with the EEOC. Interim earnings or amounts earnable with reasonable diligence shall be deducted from the back pay. But back pay may not be denied, accord-

ing to the Supreme Court, merely because of the absence of bad
faith on the part of the defendant. (Albemarle Paper Co. v. Moody,
10 FEP Cases 1181)

▶ Reinstatement or admission of a person to membership in a
union.

▶ Any other equitable relief the court deems appropriate.

The hiring, reinstatement, or admission remedies do not apply
where the respondent's action was based on any factor other than
race, color, religion, sex, or national origin.

Costs, Attorneys' Fees. Title VII allows courts discretion to
award reasonable attorneys' fees to prevailing parties — whether
plaintiff or defendant.

The Supreme Court has ruled that attorneys' fees may be
awarded to a prevailing defendant in a Title VII action upon a finding that the action was frivolous, unreasonable, or without foundation — even if it was not brought in subjective bad faith. The general standard for assessing attorneys' fees against the EEOC when
it loses a Title VII action should not be different from that applied
to private parties, the Court said. But it added that a court may consider distinctions between the EEOC and private plaintiffs in determining the reasonableness of the Commission's litigation efforts.
(Christianburg Garment Co. v. EEOC, 16 FEP Cases 502)

Compensatory Damages. One appeals court (and many district
courts) have held that compensatory damages other than those
representing back pay may not be awarded in a Title VII action.
(Pearson v. Western Electric Co., 13 FEP Cases 1202) Damages
for alleged mental distress, for example, have generally not been
awarded in Title VII actions.

Punitive Damages. The courts have divided on whether Title
VII authorizes the award of punitive damages. The majority view,
however, appears to be that such a remedy is not authorized.

In a very strong and explicit holding, the Sixth Circuit rejected
the argument that punitive damages may be awarded under Title
VII. Finding nothing in Title VII that would authorize an award of
punitive damages, the court observed that had Congress intended to
provide for this remedy, it would have done so explicitly. The court
added that, assuming punitive damages may be awarded, they may
be awarded only following a jury trial, since such damages are a
legal, rather than an equitable, remedy. (EEOC v. Detroit Edison
Co., 10 FEP Cases 239)

Regarding jury trials, the courts have held that there is no right to a jury trial under Title VII since it is aimed primarily at equitable relief. But some appeals courts have upheld the procedure of impaneling an advisory jury in Title VII cases (see Fourth Circuit holding in Cox v. Babcock & Wilcox Co., 5 FEP Cases 374; and Fifth Circuit holding in Moss v. Lane Co., 5 FEP Cases 376).

Although the courts have divided on the award of compensatory and punitive damages under Title VII, the Supreme Court held in 1975 that an individual who establishes a cause of action under both Title VII and the 1866 Act (42 U.S.C. Sec. 1981) is entitled to both equitable and legal relief, including compensatory and — in some cases — punitive damages. The remedies under the two laws are separate, distinct, and independent. (Johnson v. Railway Express Agency, 10 FEP Cases 817)

REMEDIES: PATTERN-OR-PRACTICE SUITS

In the settlement agreements with such major groups as American Telephone & Telegraph and the basic steel industry, EEOC, OFCCP, and Justice obtained broad affirmative action plans requiring the employers to upgrade employment of women and minority-group employees. These are discussed above under "Settlement Agreements."

Following a similar pattern, the Government has obtained remedies requiring broad affirmative action programs in pattern-or-practice actions against both employers and unions.

Actions Against Employers. Remedial orders in pattern-or-practice actions against employers required such affirmative action as:

▶ Filing a document listing each job classification, description of the duties, minimum salary, grade or step promotions within each classification, minimum requirements and criteria for promotions, and the persons responsible for recommending and approving promotions.

▶ Offering each job applicant the opportunity to complete an application form and providing assistance in completing it if necessary.

▶ Abstaining from giving preference in hiring to friends or relatives of employees.

▶ Posting a notice of any vacancy on a conspicuous bulletin board.

► Desegregating all facilities, including work areas, lounges, locker rooms, dressing rooms, bathrooms, and toilets.

► Making quarterly reports to the Government of all personnel actions.

Actions Against Unions. Remedial orders in pattern-or-practice actions against unions have also been broad. In one case, the union was ordered to admit members immediately on a nondiscriminatory basis and to develop new admission standards following nondiscriminatory principles. It also was ordered to refer for jobs alternately "one black and one white, so long as there are available persons of both races who have applied." (See U.S. v. Local 53, Asbestos Workers, 1 FEP Cases 577.)

Reverse Discrimination Problems. Affirmative action programs often raise the problem of "reverse discrimination." In attempting to eradicate the effects of past discrimination, a program may have the effect of discriminating against presently employed white males. Decisions involving this issue are discussed above under "Reverse Discrimination."

REPORTS, RECORDS

Under Section 709(c) of Title VII, EEOC has authority to require covered employers, employment agencies, and labor unions to keep and preserve records and to file reports.

In addition, Section 709(a) of Title VII gives EEOC access to and the right to copy any "evidence" of a person proceeded against or investigated. But the right to copy is limited to evidence that relates to prescribed unfair employment practices and that is relevant to a charge under investigation by EEOC.

There are provisions for granting exemptions from the record-keeping and reporting requirements in cases of undue hardship. There also are statutory exemptions for those required to keep records or file reports under a state or local law or an Executive Order of the U.S. Government. Moreover, it is unlawful for EEOC to make public information from the records that are required to be kept.

EEOC requires an employer to keep for six months all personnel records that are made. The records that must be kept are those made in connection with job applications, hiring, promotion, demotion, transfer, layoffs, rates of pay, other forms of compensation, and selection for apprenticeship or training. If an employee is discharged, the employer must keep his personnel records for six months from the date of discharge.

Records Kept by Employers. The records that must be kept by employers include the following:

► All personnel records that are made. But an employer need not keep application forms and other preemployment records of applicants for seasonal or temporary jobs.

► A copy of the employer report form (EEO-1) that was filed most recently.

► Postemployment records. Where such records are kept, EEOC suggests that they be kept separate from basic personnel records, and they may be incorporated in an automatic data processing system in the payroll department.

► A list of applicants who wish to participate in apprenticeship programs. The list must be kept in the chronological order in which the applications are received. It also should include the address of each applicant and a notation of his or her sex and identification of race or national origin. The list must be kept for two years or the period of a successful applicant for apprenticestip, whichever is longer.

Union Records. All local unions with 100 or more members must make and keep records that are necessary for completing EEOC report form EEO-3. These records must be kept for one year from the due date of the report.

"Referral" unions must preserve other membershp or referral records, including applications for six months from the date of the making of the record.

State, Local Governments. Under the 1972 amendments, state and local jurisdictions with 100 or more employees are required annually to file report form EEO-4 covering employment by minority group, sex, occupation, and salary range.

There also are recordkeeping rules for elementary and secondary schools. Under EEOC rules, public and secondary school systems, districts, and individual schools with 15 or more employees must keep personnel and employment records for two years and employment statistics by race and job category for three years. In addition, school systems that employ 100 or more employees must file EEO-5 reporting forms annually.

EEOC's right to require states to submit these forms has been upheld by the First Circuit. (United States v. State of New Hampshire, 13 FEP Cases 654)

Forms Required. EEOC has seven forms that must be filed.

► EEO-1 must be filed by all employers covered by Title VII that have 100 or more employees and by government contractors covered by Executive Order 11246 that have 50 or more employees and government contracts of $50,000 or more.

► EEO-2 must be filed annually by joint labor-management committees that have five or more trainees in their programs and at least one employer and union sponsor covered by Title VII.

► EEO-2-E must be filed annually by employers operating unilateral apprenticeship programs. But programs with four or less apprentices need not be reported. The form must be filed by each employer who has a company-wide employment of 100 or more employees and who conducts and controls an employer-operated apprenticeship program with four or more apprentices.

► EEO-3 must be filed annually by local unions that have 100 or more members at any time since the previous December 31. An international union is not required to file a report unless it operates a local union under a trusteeship or other arrangement.

► EEO-4 must be filed annually by state and local governmental jurisdictions with 100 or more employees.

► EEO-5 must be filed annually by public and secondary school systems, districts, and individual schools with 15 or more employees.

► EEO-6 must be filed biennially by every institution of higher learning with 15 or more employees.

In addition to giving the EEOC the authority to require the filing reports, Title VII authorizes the EEOC to require the posting of a prescribed notice setting forth summaries of pertinent provisions of the Act and information relating to the filing of a complaint.

TABLE OF CASES

109

INDEX